Vintage Upcycling

With Raspberry Pi and Arduino

Enrico Miglino

Table of Content

Preface

A lot of fun and challenging too

The Shed magazine is predominantly a print magazine and we have been privileged to have published most of the articles here in this publication by Enrico Miglino.

These upcycling projects have been very well received by our readers who enjoy their spare time, making and creating projects for fun or folly. With electronics now playing such a huge, huge part in our everyday lives, so many more of our readers are enjoying projects of this type where they can test their skills and expand their knowledge horizons.

All these projects here do just that and we hope you enjoy them as much as our readers have. To test your skills and have fun doing so is the perfect way to enjoy your leisure time. There is nothing like creating a project that brings on a smile and makes good use of stylish antique pieces while using contemporary, easy to access, hardware and software.

These upcycling projects are a perfect match for the electronics hobbyist and for those that appreciate that many older items still have value, use and a place with us all in the 21st century.

Enjoy.

Greg Vincent, Publishing editor
The Shed magazine

Acknowledgments

If you are reading this book it is also thanks to the support and sponsorship of Project14 and the element14.com community that gave me the possibility and help to create the three part workshop "Vintage Upcycling". During the chats with Tariq while preparing the workshop script, I had the idea of writing this book.

A big thanks also to Greg and The Shed magazine where I published some of the projects covered by this work.

The presentation of professional schematics and PCB designs was made possible thanks to the kind sponsorship of Altium Designer, one of the best CAD circuit design applications.

All the 3D printed components shown in these projects were made using filament and resin 3D printers provided by Elegoo.

Introduction

by Tariq Ahmad

Community manager of Project14 at element14.com

When I think of vintage electronics, what I tend to think of the beautiful craftsmanship on my parents old Marentz receiver from the 70s accompanied with floor speakers with room filling sound. Or, maybe a vintage console television with a CRT screen that was 25 inches, which was bulky even by today's standards, even if the screen is smaller than what people are use to. Technology back then was not meant to be tucked away or hidden, it had to be made as beautiful as any piece of furniture in the room. Nowadays, the life cycle for electronics is much shorter, and the footprint it leaves is not so drastic.

When Enrico, approached me about doing a workshop around an old rotary phone, I recalled a rotary phone that I fell in love with at a neighbours house growing up. Bringing back something old and familiar, isn't just a shameless plug for nostalgia, it's a return to something beauty lost. For all its sophistication, today's technology has a short life cycle, and an almost disposable quality. This was less the case 40 or 50 years ago, has time flown by so much since then? The upcycling workshop that Enrico proposed, felt almost Proustian, in its search for time regained. Every piece of vintage technology recalled memories from era lost but not forgotten.

The idea for having workshops on the element14 community came from a desire to make electronics projects accessible to everyone. That was one of the missions of the Project14 project competitions held on the element14 community. With Enrico's support, we got together to arrange a series of workshops based on projects in this book, that involved upcycling Vintage Electronics.

What is upcycling you might ask? Upcycling, also known as creative reuse of existing material or products perceived to be of great quality or aesthetic value. For electronics hobbyists, that usually means using something like a Raspberry Pi or an Arduino, in order to make something old, new again. The idea for the Vintage Tech Workshop.

The idea for this workshop was to inspire people to take cool vintage appliances and repurpose them using a Raspberry Pi or an Arduino. If you are a fan of electronics, you likely have some older electronics lying around that are in need of a second life. One of the goals of upcycling is to prevent wasting material that could be potentially useful by making use of it. By doing so, you reduce the consumption of new raw materials in effect creating a new product; thus, reducing energy usage, air and water pollution, and even greenhouse gas emissions.

Following the 3 part workshop series on Vintage Upcycling with Raspberry Pi and Arduino that Enrico hosted, the members voted on a Recycle & Retrofit competition in the Project14 program on element14 community. Project14, is a member-driven program on the element14 community where members come up with ideas for competitions, vote on the competitions they want to participate in, and then decide the winners of those competitions. In fact, the first competition ever run on Project14 was Techno Toys, an upcycling competition, and throughout the programs lifespan, many of the most memorable electronics projects, involved upcycling.

Upcycling connects the past to present in a way that honours what we cherish from vintage electronics while improving it to make it contemporary using modern electronics such as a Pi or an Arduino. One of the goals of upcycling is have a more "creative" version of recycling, not only designing, adapting and making usable something vintage, while adding more value, and a brand-new charm. To "upcycle" an item, is to essentially update, modernise or deconstruct it. Upcycling is about aesthetics as well as substance. Upcycling can make what you once loved, contemporary while not losing any of its old world charm.

If you're new to electronics projects, or upcycling, we hope this book inspires you to try your hand in electronics project. If you're more experienced, we hope that the projects in this book inspire you to take on an upcycling project and make something beautiful. In this way we can make what is old, new and sustainable at the same time.

## CHAPTER 1

Upcycling a 1970 Desk Lamp

1.1 Introduction

This project first appeared on "The Shed" magazine issue number 88, January/February 2020 (https://the-shed.nz/)

Repository link: https://github.com/alicemirror/LampUpcycling

This is one of the first upcycling projects I published on The Shed magazine; the selected vintage appliance I decided to revive is a Brionvega desk lamp, an iconic Italian design appliance by the mid-'70s. When I bought this lamp, the device got me a special feeling, so I decided to upcycle it trying to make something better, up to date with the contemporary technology, but leaving intact the original stylish sensation.

In cases when the project is relatively easy in terms of electronics, working on an old device avoiding to interfere as much as possible with its original aspect makes the project quite complex.

An upcycling project needs using the space available inside the device without adding – where possible – any external parts, components or making drastic changes. The removal of the unused original components inside should not compromise the structure and the functionality: minimal aesthetic changes to the structure are a must.

This is what I figured out when I saw the lamp on the shelf of a vintage shop.

1.2 Design and Circuit

I decided to change the lighting features of the lamp, adding a sensing device and a linear regulator of the light intensity. The digital control of the new features can be easily reached with an Arduino board; due to the limited space available inside the base of the lamp, I opted for an *Arduino Nano*.

As a matter of fact, the Nano version includes the same characteristics of the traditional *Arduino UNO* and the same GPIO pins, but with a reduced form factor.

One of the most important aspects of this upcycling project is the dramatic reduction of the power consumption of the device itself, providing better lighting, transforming the appliance from analog to digital.

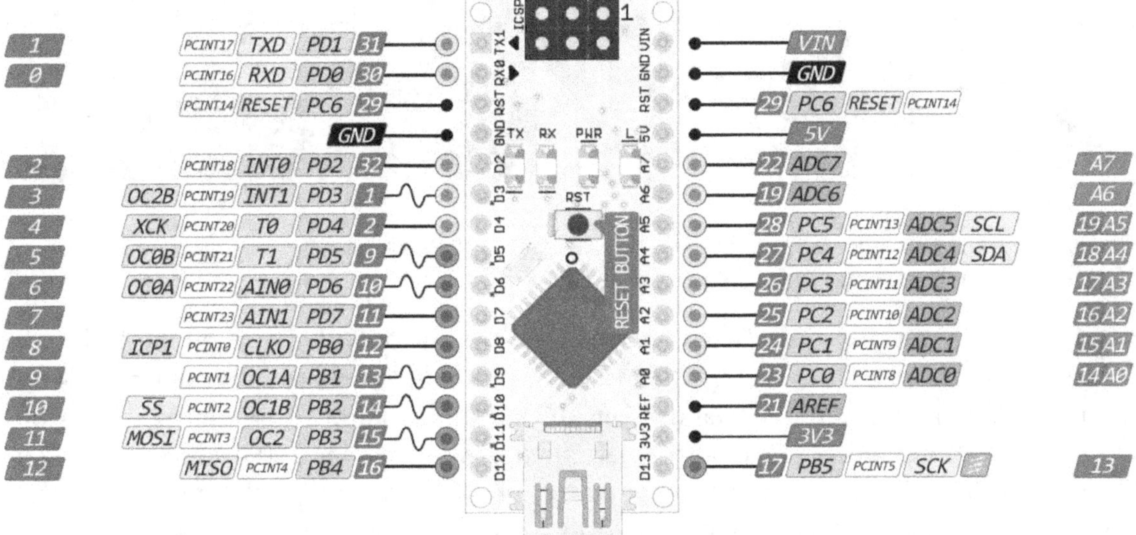

The complete Pinout of the Arduino Nano GPIO. Many pins of the board can be used for different features, as well as coming digital I/O pins.

A technical problem I had to test before deciding the reliability of the entire project was the use of a set of high-efficiency low-power LEDs to replace the original yellowish 12V lamp. One of the bigger differences between almost any kind of electronic device produced after the mid of past century compared with the modern ones is the working voltage and power consumption.

At least until the end of '80s, the low voltage for lamps, radios, and a lot of electronic devices was 12V; the new version of the Brionvega lamp should work instead of a voltage of 5V. Not only, but I wanted to power it with a standard USB port: this means keeping the power needed for the entire circuit under 500 mA.

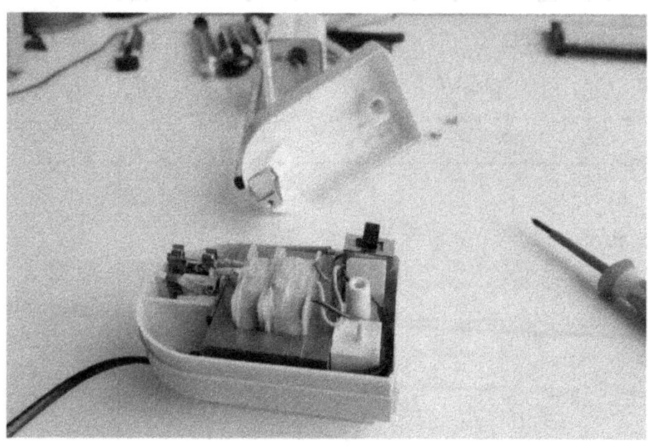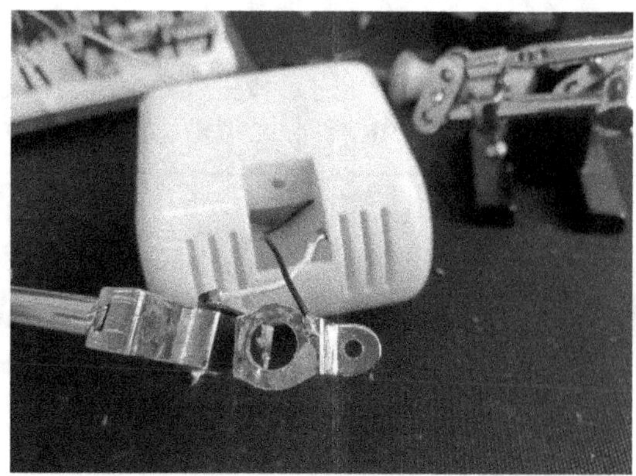

To the left, the base lamp with the original parts that should be removed.
To the right, the head lamp holder also removed.

I decided to make a grid of 12 white LEDs to provide good lighting; all the LEDs are connected in parallel to an *NPN 2N2222* transistor, acting as a micro relay controlled by an Arduino PWM output pin and eventually amplifying the Arduino 5V output powering the LEDs. After testing the power required, I verified that is sufficient 104 mA for the whole circuit with the light set at the maximum power; good, a standard USB connection to any device (laptop, smartphone, portable power bank, USB charger) should work fine.

I decided to make a grid of 12 white LEDs to provide good lighting; all the LEDs are connected in parallel to an *NPN 2N2222* transistor, acting as a micro relay controlled by an Arduino PWM output pin and eventually amplifying the Arduino 5V output powering the LEDs. After testing the power required, I verified that is sufficient 104 mA for the whole circuit with the light set at the maximum power; good, a standard USB connection to any device (laptop, smartphone, portable power bank, USB charger) should work fine.

To test the parts of the circuit and programming the Arduino Nano before assembling the new version of the lamp, I made a full working prototype on a breadboard, accordingly with the circuit design.

The first step was opening the lamp and removing the original bulb and the power supply on the base, an internal 220V AC to 12V DC transformer controlled by an on/off switch. After removing the transformer – the bigger component of the lamp – almost all the base box was empty for the new installation.

The circuit design, and the 3D printable STL files of the project, as well as the Arduino software, are available on GitHub.

I have also added an electret microphone to be used as a tap sensor for the light. The sensor, together with the Arduino Nano assembled on a small breadboard PCB and the slider, and a power switch, are all the components I used. These fit inside the lamp base; the assembly of the internal new components was hot-glued to keep them in place.

The switch selector to enable or disable the electret microphone tap sensor instead is accessible by the exterior of the base on the bottom side. The position of the switch is the less impacting one and does not alter the aesthetic of the lamp design.

After testing and building the 3D components on a breadboard, I used them to develop the Arduino sketch I proceeded with the assembly of the upcycled device.

1.3 3D Printing the New Parts

The LEDs grid support replacing the original lamp bulb should fit in the rounded rectangle of the lamp head, while a slider button will replace the original on/off switch on the lamp base. To make these objects, designed with Fusion360, I used the Elegoo LCD resin 3D printer to produce smoother and good shaped objects, instead of using a traditional PLA filament printer.

The resin 3D printer provides a smaller printing volume compared to the 200x200x200 mm of the filament printer but can reach a precision of 0,05 mm or less, almost a factor 10 respect the fusion filament technology I use to 3D print bigger parts.

3D rendering of the LEDs grid support in the lamp head.

To keep an eye to the environmental impact, for the first time I used the brand new Elegoo washable grey resin; while this product has the same quality of the traditional resin, the 3D prints can be cleaned using water, drastically reducing the pollution problems of cleaning the parts with Isopropyl alcohol, that need to be treated in a special way instead of just discard the residues at home, cleaned with water.

1.4 Assembling the Lamp

The LEDs Grid

According to the circuit, the <u>12 LEDs</u> connected in parallel to the 2N2222 transistor have a limiting resistor connected to the Vcc side, driven by the transistor.

After hot-gluing the LEDs in the respective holes of the 3D printed support on the backside I have soldered the limiting resistors and the led terminals in parallel. In this way, only two wires should be connected to the circuit in the base of the lamp.

To wire the LEDs grid in the lamp head to the base hosting the Arduino Nano and the rest of the circuit I have reused the original extensible pole of the lamp; the external metallic part of the pole is connected to the ground while an internal wire is connected to the VCC.

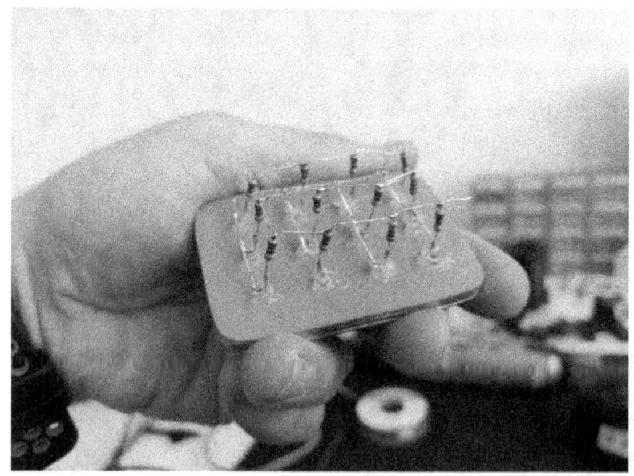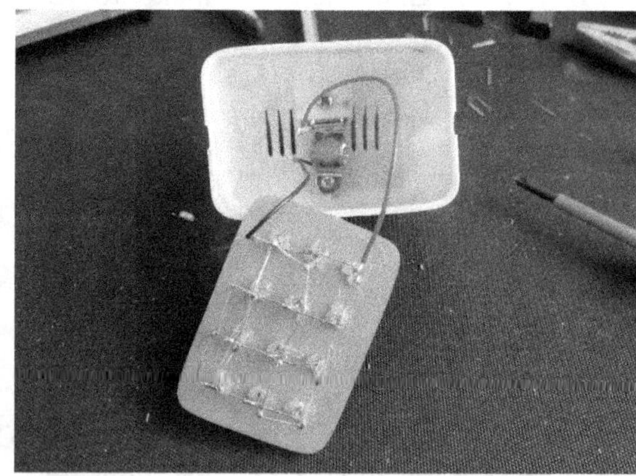

The LEDs grid with the two terminals soldered to the extensible pole, inside of the lamp head.

The Lamp Base

The Arduino Nano has been soldered on a small piece of prototyping PCB hosting the rest of the circuit.

After soldering the LEDs wires to the base of the extensive pole I connected the power supply of the Arduino Nano through a USB cable; reusing the lamp 220 VAC power cable hole, the upcycled device can be powered by the USB output of a computer or a USB charger.

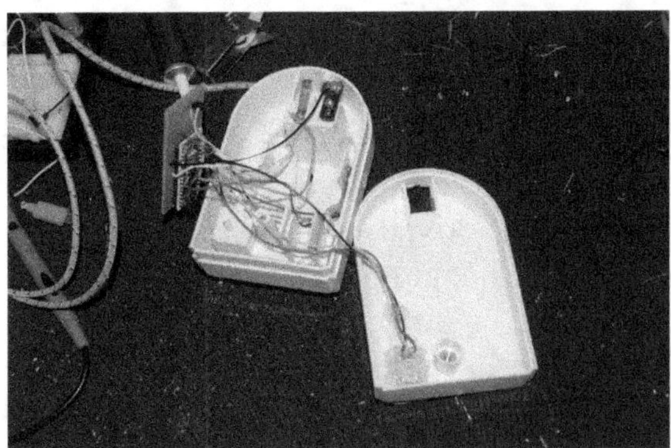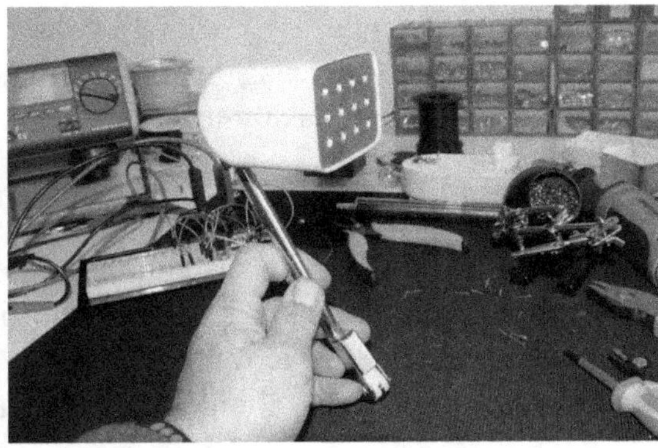

The lamp base hosting the Arduino Nano and the new components (left) and the upcycled lamp head (right) with the LEDs grid.

1.5 From Analog to Digital Lighting

The software architecture of the sketch is quite simple to follow.

```
#define MIN_DIMMER 30        ///< Minimum analog value of the potentiometer
#define MAX_DIMMER 255       ///< Maximum analog value of the potentiometer
#define OFF_LIGHT 0         ///< Light intensity off
#define LOW_LIGHT 50        ///< Light intensity min range
#define HIGH_LIGHT 255       ///< Light intensity max tange
#define RESPONSIVITY 50      ///< Sensitivity of the dimmer readings in ms
//!  The sample window amplitude of 50 ms correspond to a frequency of 20 Hz
#define SAMPLE_FREQ 50
#define MIC_TRIGGER 400      ///< Min sampled value to trig the light
```

I defined a series of constants to drive the behaviour of the program and control the limits of the dimmer and the tap sensor. These values were deducted empirically and refer to this specific kind of appliance; it is not difficult to replicate the same behaviour in a different container of a different kind of lamp just reconfiguring the values.

MIN_DIMMER and MAX_DIMMER depends on the effective potentiometer range and corresponds to the analog values read on both extremes of the slider.

The three constants OFF_LIGHT MIN_LIGHT and MAX_LIGHT instead define the range of the LEDs intensity provided by the PWM (Pulse-With-Modulation) output pin that controls the light power transistor. The Off status should always be zero, used to power off the lamp while the Min and Max value depends on the kind of LEDs used, as well as the number of LEDs connected in parallel.

The MIC_TRIGGER constant instead defines the sound level that the electret microphone should detect to switch the light on/off. We should note that when I tested the software on the breadboard prototype the sensitivity of the microphone was higher than in the final assembly where the microphone is inside the lamp base. Depending on the thickness of the container the sensibility should be configured accordingly.

The sketch source available on GitHub includes the USB to Serial interface initialisation in the setup function and commands in the loop function for testing the values with the Serial Terminal available on the Arduino IDE, I used to define the ranges defined in the constants described above. The code of the serial interface can be deleted as it is for testing and debug purposes only and does not impact on the logic of the sketch.

```
// ------------------------------------------------------------
// --------- Check for the dimmer current position
// ------------------------------------------------------------
// As the analog value is between 0 and 1023, it should be
// mapped to the limits of the min/max light PWM value
// Before mapping we check if the values are outside the dimmer range
// to set the off and max intensity mode without flickering
if(dimmer <= MIN_DIMMER) {
    intensity = OFF_LIGHT;
} else if(dimmer >= MAX_DIMMER) {
        intensity = HIGH_LIGHT;
} else {
    intensity = map(dimmer, MIN_DIMMER, MAX_DIMMER, LOW_LIGHT, HIGH_LIGHT);
}
```

The first part of the loop function – executed at every cycle – checks if the light control (the slider potentiometer, or dimmer) changed its position. According to the analog value of dimmer, the corresponding intensity value is calculated, mapping the dimmer range to the intensity levels range: the dimmer range corresponds to the analog values read from the analog input A0, while the intensity level corresponds to the PWM value set to the output pin connected to the transistor.

Note that if the dimmer value is under the lower range the lamp intensity is set to zero (light off), while if the value is higher than the max value the intensity is set to the max value. This solution avoids the light flickering when set to off or to the higher intensity.

The second part is controlled by the sensor activation switch.

```
if(digitalRead(MIC_CONTROL_PIN) == true) {
    [Electret microphone tap sensor reading]
    }
```

If the switch pin defined on the GPIO by the MIC_CONTROL_PIN is set to on, the updated light intensity level is applied only if the user who taps the microphone sensor has powered the lamp, otherwise the light intensity level is forced to zero (light off)

The light intensity is set every cycle with the PWM instruction

```
analogWrite(LIGHT_PIN, intensity);
```

The only complex part of this sketch is the Electret microphone tap sensor reading. Let me have a look at a step back to see how the software works when a Tap is detected on the MIC_CONTROL_PIN GPIO input port.

```
// collect data for 50 mS and save the max and min values
    while ( (millis() - startMillis) < sampleWindow ) {
        // Check sample
        sample = analogRead(A1);
        if (sample < MAX_SIGNAL) {
            if (sample > signalMax) {
            signalMax = sample;
                } else if (sample < signalMin) {
                    signalMin = sample;
                } // Smaller than las saved min
```

```
        } // Greater than last saved max
    } // while ... sample cycle

// Calculate the peak-to-peak amplitude of the last sample.
// If the amplitude reach the trigger level, the status of the light
// is changed
peakToPeak = abs(signalMax - signalMin);

// Reset the min/max values
signalMax  = 0;
signalMin = MAX_SIGNAL;

// Check if the light status should be changed
if(peakToPeak > MIC_TRIGGER) {
    // Change the light status
    if(lightStatus == true) {
        // Bypass the intensity value read from the slider
        // and force the value to off
        lightStatus = false; // Update the status of the light
        // Update the light
        analogWrite(LIGHT_PIN, 0);
    } else {
        lightStatus = true;  // Update the status of the light
    }
} // Mic sampling is triggered
// Update the light status if the light is on. This is to accept
// light intensity changes also when the mic sensor is active.
if(lightStatus == true) {
    // Update the light
    analogWrite(LIGHT_PIN, intensity);
}
```

The electret microphone provides an amplified voltage read by the analog input port A1 corresponding to the intensity of the detected sound frequency. In order to detect a "tap" from the user, a single reading is not sufficient, so I adopted a sampling method to grant the reliability of the readings.

Every loop cycle, if the MIC_CONTROL_PIN detects the tap sensor enabled a series of readings is started for the duration of 50 ms. During this period, the higher and lower intensity levels are saved on the two variables signalMin and signalMax.

As the cycle ends, the absolute value of the difference is calculated: the obtained value indicates if a consistent sound variation has been detected and accordingly with the peakToPeak amplitude if the value is greater than the MIC_TRIGGER value the light status is toggled between on/off.

Through MIC_TRIGGER it is possible to change the sensitivity of the microphone. The lamp can be configured to react to a variation of the environment sound or a particular range of frequencies.

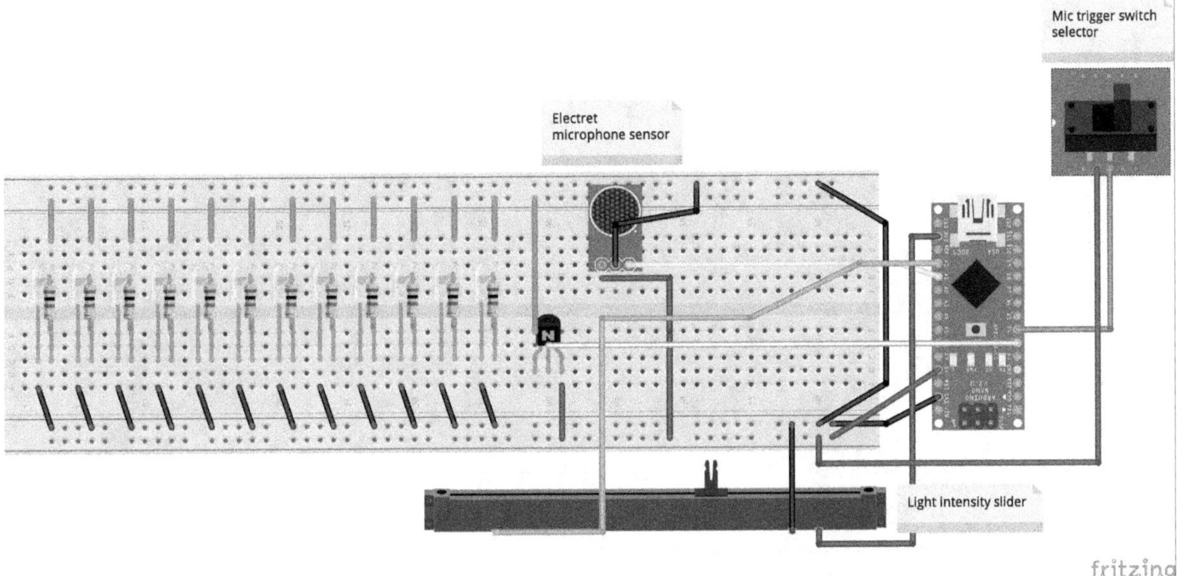

Schematics of the essential elements with wiring notes to set the LEDs array working in both modes: activated by the sound sensor or with fixed light.

## CHAPTER 2

New Life for a Yokogawa Milliampere Meter

2.1 The Story

This project first appeared on "The Shed" magazine issue number 87, September/October 2019 (https://the-shed.nz/)

Repository link: https://github.com/alicemirror/yokogawa

When I found a YOKOGAWA milliampere meter dated 1972 circa I was not sure what to do with it, but it was in very good conditions so I decided to buy it on the second-hand market.

After a good cleaning to the Bakelite case, I tried to see how it was working measuring the low power levels of an Arduino connected to an RGB LED. As the gauge of the milliampere meter worked fine but with a lower sensibility than expected, I removed the coil from inside and repeated the test, getting a better result.

Then, I focused my efforts on the options available for a new project: the YOKOGAWA upcycling.

Due to the available space inside the case after removing the measuring coil, for this project I decided to use an Arduino UNO. The idea is to show the interaction of the device with the environment sounds and loudness generating some visual effects with lights and a consistent motion of the milliampere meter gauge.

The Yokogawa milliampere meter (first light test).

A considerable portion of the front face of the case is occupied by the analogue gauge: a big light panel, perfect to host a suggestive visual effect with some Neopixel strips, easy to control with a single Arduino pin and the Adafruit Neopixel library.

One of the nice things I find in the vintage electronic devices is the incredible amount of free space you can get by removing the components that are not necessary for the upcycling project. The design of some decades ago did not pay much attention to the internal space optimisation of the devices, a useful factor when redesigning their functionalities.

The environment sound interaction can be produced reading the variations detected by an electret microphone sensor connected to the Arduino board.

Most of the space inside the milliampere meter was occupied by the copper coil, the component to use the same gauge with four kinds of measurement ranges.

The new space after removing the coil hosts the Arduino UNO and the wires connected to the gauge.

These kinds of sensors present the advantage of including an extra digital signal triggering a preset level. When the audio level is triggered, the corresponding audio analog value from the microphone sensor can be read by the Arduino UNO board. The detected audio level is converted in light colour and intensity.

It is sufficient to wire in-series to the LED strips power line the milliampere meter gauge to get a measure.

As a matter of fact, the gauge moves accordingly to the different colours and light intensity of the Neopixel strips; every kind of colour consumes a different power that can be registered by the milliampere meter: measuring this kind of values if just the job of the device.

2.2 Rethinking the Device

The upcycling process is also the art of using what we find (inside the vintage objects), and this upcycling process is the perfect example.

To make the job I figured out with this milliampere meter, I noted some important details that proved to be very useful to keep intact the external aspect while applying changes.

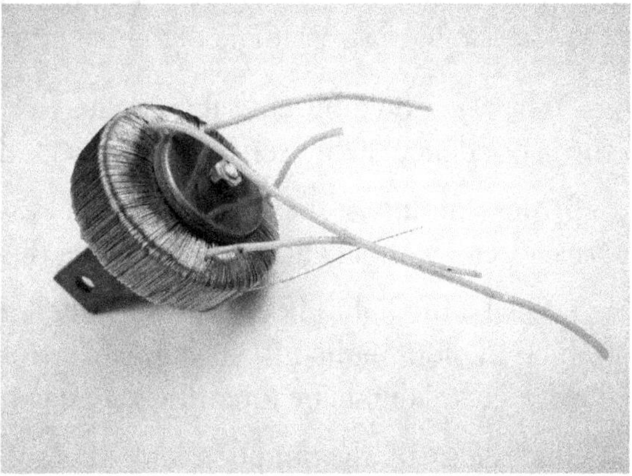

Internal view of the milliampere meter (left) and the big measure coil removed (right).

Removing the Coil

The first operation I did was to remove the big copper coil from inside of the box; this is used to adapt up to four different measures ranges with the same gauge.

After removing the coil, I soldered a couple of wires directly to the gauge terminations; these wires will be used for measuring the power consumed by the Neopixel LEDs.

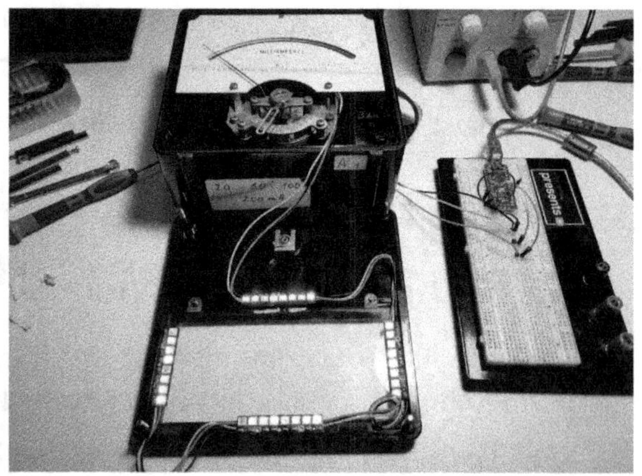

New wires soldered to the internal side of the measuring clamps (left) and the Neopixel light strips wired to the internal frame of the front panel (right).

To measure on different value ranges the same coil was connected to four wires, soldered in correspondence of different turns connected to the four terminal clamps.

By desoldering all the coil wires I got easy access from the external side of the box to the internal circuit without adding any extra modification.

To make the light effect I disassembled the front panel of the milliampere meter; then I hot-glued the four eight-LEDs Neopixel strips. These are hidden by the black Bakelite frame of the device, to illuminate the white gauge panel.

Regardless of the number and kind of Neopixel elements, these can be connected together and and controlled by a single Arduino GPIO pin.

This approach makes it easy to create the light and colour effect coming from the black frame of the milliampere meter directed to the gauge panel.

The External Sound Sensor

The electret microphone sensor has four wires: Vcc, GND, the digital trigger signal, and the analogue sensor level. The whole sensor is assembled on a small PCB that I soldered on one side of a small prototyping PCB.

Then on the same PCB, I also added an orange LED as visual feedback of the trigger. By including the LED connection I needed five wires, exactly the five clamps available on the top of the milliampere meter!

To make the installation more suggestive I used a couple of coloured spring-bended wires on the external. To fix stable the PCB sensor to the top clamps I bent two pieces of bicycle spokes connected to the two power wires, fixed to the two rightmost clamps by one side and soldered to the PCB to the other.

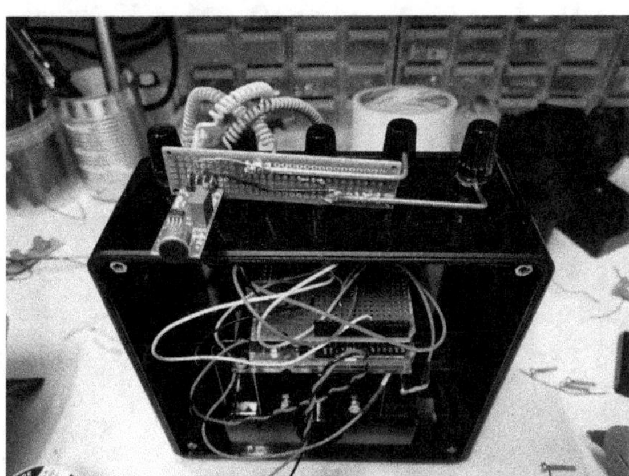
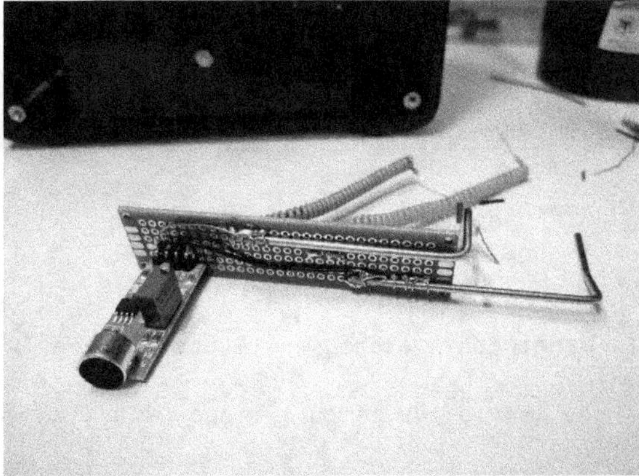

Internal view of the upcycled milliampere meter (left) and the sound sensor soldered on the custom PCB board (right).

2.3 The Software

The logic of the software is divided into two parts: the Neopixel control functions and the analogue data acquisition from the microphone.

The globals.h header file defines the constants and parameters to control the software behaviour.

```c
struct Rainbow {
int intensity; ///< Light intensity, set accordingly with the last sound level reading
long firstPixelHue; ///< The first pixel hue value of the rainbow rotating sequence
};


// Audio sensor constants
#define SENSOR_ANALOG A0 ///< Arduino input pin to accept the Sound Sensor's analog
output
#define SENSOR_DIGITAL 3 ///< Arduino input pin to accept the Sound Sensor's digital
output
#define SENSOR_LED 4 ///< LED for direct soundsensor feedback


/**
* The sensor sensitivity level is the Analog value (around the mid of the 10 bits of the
AD Arduino port)
* You can set this value accoridngly with the environmental conditions where the sensor
should work.
* Alternatively, a potentiometer on analog input A1 can be used to dynamically control the
final
* sensitivity level that is the analog level triggering the LED.
*/
#define SENSOR_SENSITIVITY 520


/**
* Delay between two samples. Every cycle between the samplea sueinf wcwey loop cycle. This
delay
* is applied to the timed tRainbow funciton that executes one step (with this delay)
everytime
* it is called.
*/
#define SAMPLE_INTERVAL 3


//! Neopixel constants
#define NEOPIXEL_PIN 6 ///< Neopixel signal pin
//! Number of Neopixel LEDs in the strip (four sequential 8 LEDs strips)
#define NEOPIXEL_LEDS 32
//! Minimum light intensity (absolute min = 0)
#define LIGHT_MIN 5
//! Maximum light intensity (absolute max = 255)
#define LIGHT_MAX 50
```

The Rainbow structure collects the sensor data and saves the current LED colour range. The colour change is controlled by the function stepRainbow().

```
/**
 * Rainbow cycle along whole strip.
 *
 * The function executes a single rainbow step, controlled by the Rainbow
 * globla structure. The funcion is a single-step event to be interruptable
 * inside a more conplex cycle.
 */
void stepRainbow() {
// Set the intensity accordingly with the last sensor reading
strip.setBrightness(rainbowControl.intensity);

// Execute a rainbow step
for(int i = 0; i < strip.numPixels(); i++) { // For each pixel in strip...
  // Offset pixel hue by an amount to make one full revolution of the
  // color wheel (range of 65536) along the length of the strip
  // (strip.numPixels() steps):
  int pixelHue = rainbowControl.firstPixelHue + (i * 65536L / strip.numPixels());
  // strip.ColorHSV() can take 1 or 3 arguments: a hue (0 to 65535) or
  // optionally add saturation and value (brightness) (each 0 to 255).
  // Here we're using just the single-argument hue variant. The result
  // is passed through strip.gamma32() to provide 'truer' colors
  // before assigning to each pixel:
  strip.setPixelColor(i, strip.gamma32(strip.ColorHSV(pixelHue)));
 }
 strip.show(); // Update strip with new contents
}
```

The Adafruit Neopixel library provides a series of examples; I made a modified, and interactive version of the rainbow() library function in the Arduino sketch. The modified function stepRainbow() does not interrupt the cycle while shading the LEDs colours but executes a new step inside the main loop() function.

The original function, instead, sets a predefined light intensity value, then cycles continuously a smooth rainbow sequence along with the LEDs (here I use 32 LEDs from four strips of eight connected sequentially) blocking the execution of the main loop until it ends.

```
void loop(){
 analogValue = analogRead(SENSOR_ANALOG);
 digitalValue = digitalRead(SENSOR_DIGITAL);

 if(digitalValue == HIGH) {
  // Just trigger the LED
  digitalWrite(SENSOR_LED, HIGH);
 }
 else {
  // Check the detected value and trigger the LED accordingly
  if(analogValue > SENSOR_SENSITIVITY) {
   digitalWrite(SENSOR_LED,HIGH);
   } else {
    digitalWrite(SENSOR_LED,LOW);
   }
 }

 updateIntensity();
 updateRainbowPixel();
 stepRainbow();
 delay(SAMPLE_INTERVAL); // Slight pause so that we don't overwhelm the serial interface
}
```

To make the light cycle interactive accordingly to the audio level I split the rainbow() function showing a single light rotation step every loop() cycle.

Together with the call of the function every loop() cycle the microphone level is checked to see if the audio has changed by the last reading and the light intensity is updated accordingly.

To make the audio sensor-I have used a prototyping PCB connected to the five wire-clamps of the milliampere meter; the circuit also includes an orange LED blinking when the preset microphone sensibility level is triggered, so the user can regulate it depending on the global audio level of the environment with a small screwdriver.

The full software sources are available on GitHub.

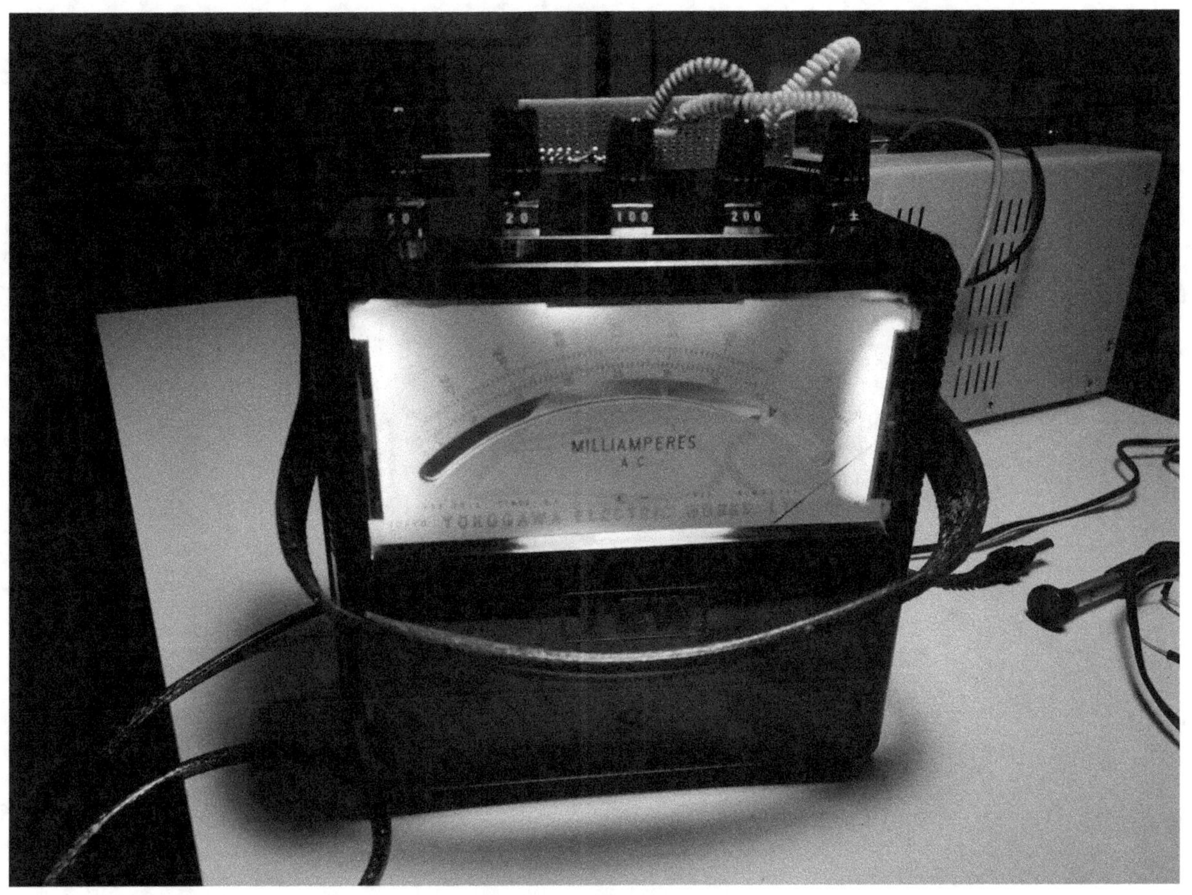

The finished upcycled Yokogawa milliampere meter in action.

CHAPTER 3

The Pi Rotary

3.1 Introduction

This project first appeared on "The Shed" magazine issue number 89, March/April 2020 (https://the-shed.nz/) and has been introduced in the first Project14 workshop "Vintage Upcycling" by https://www.element14.com/community/community/project14/acoustics/blog/2020/03/01/the-pi-rotary

Repository link: https://github.com/alicemirror/PiRotary

The Pi Rotary moves a step ahead in the class of projects of this book. Regardless of the simplicity of the technology of the device – a mid-'60s rotary phone – this upcycling work required more time then I expected.

Together with a Raspberry Pi and a few other components, making all the new features working as desired was a challenging and fascinating experience.

When I started working on the Pi Rotary project I was already aware of what to expect opening this nice piece of past. But that didn't make the job easier.

Every time I start changing the behaviour of a vintage object, frequently adding or replacing some original parts with the most recent technologies, it is like to travel with a time machine, take something from the past jumping it to the future. In this case, a rotary phone made up a jump over half a century.

The 1960' rotary telephone upcycled in this project.

Regardless of the aesthetic of the models the technology of the rotary phones remained the same for decades.

We can identify the rotary dial – an electro-mechanic component used to generate the phone number – the bell ringer, activated by a solenoid, and a hangout switch enabled when the pickup takes to start a phone call. Part of the rotary phone is the pickup including a carbon speaker on the hearing side and a small electrostatic microphone to the opposite side.

The rotary phone is a voice terminal.

When the pickup is removed from its position the phone is connected to the wired phone network and the nearest distribution box connected to it a typical line frequency is generated.

At this point the user dial the desired number, corresponding to a remote analogue device.

The Rotary System

The phone rotary dial generates a different number of pulses depending on the number: from 1 for the number 1 up to 9 for the number 9 while the number 0 corresponds to 10 pulses.

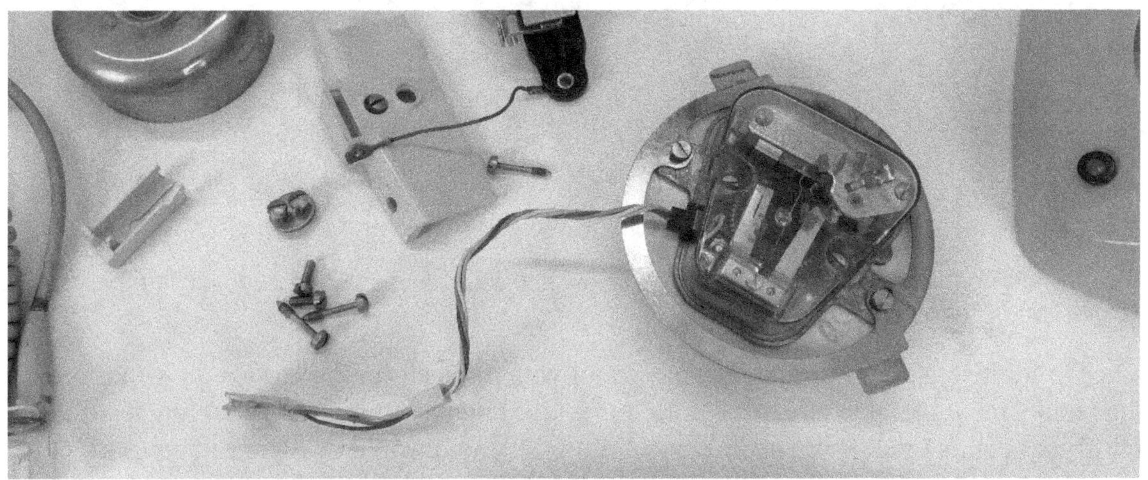

The rotary machine switching system has been an automatic telephone exchange connection produced in Europe from the year 1910. This system was based on electro-mechanic relay boxes able to select a specific user based on the number composed with the rotary dial.

This is the most important part of the Pi Rotary project because I used this component as the User Interface to access and control the new features.

Other parts of the telephone, instead, like the bell ringer and the solenoid, as well as the original circuit have been removed to make space to the new components.

With some effort, I was able to pack inside the telephone a Raspberry Pi with a PiJuice battery, a small amplifier with its rechargeable battery and the custom shield circuit controlled by the software.

3.2 Removing the Unwanted Parts

The bell is triggered by the vibration of a small metal hammer connected to a solenoid working at a relatively high voltage.

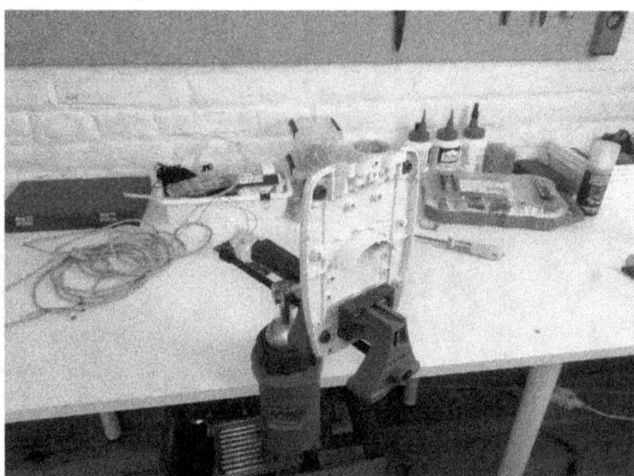

Disassembling the content of the telephone body (left) and the base while removing the plastic protection of the ring bell (right).

On the telephone board, an analog circuit with a transformer provides the voltage from the phone line cable. It would be possible to reverse engineer this circuit adapting it with 5V, but the risk is that the power needed to work the solenoid would be higher than what can be provided by the circuit

The group of the metal bell, the ringer hammer, and the solenoid have been removed easily but it was not possible to completely remove the circuit PCB with the discrete components because the custom-shaped PCB is also the support of the pickup switch. For first, I desoldered and removed all the components from the board taking care to avoid to destroy the original e PCB wires.

After cleaning the PCB and removing everything but the pickup switch support, with a tested I found two points of the circuit there detect the switch status where I soldered two wires to be used later.

The pickup switch, in fact, remained one of the essential functional parts and should continue to do its job: detecting when the pickup is taken by the user.

After disassembling the telephone and removing the ring bell components, I cut the plastic support of the bell to free more space and leave a semi-circular space to the bottom base to get a better heating dissipation of the Raspberry Pi. I hdid this operation with a Dremel cutting tool; removing the plastic part I got the base completely flat while recovering all the possible space available.

After this operation, the pickup switch becomes a common temporary switch in a strategic position.

3.3 Preparing the Pickup

I converted the phone pickup into a couple of small stereo speakers. To do this job I used a cheap Bluetooth amplifier also including a 3.5 mm audio-in jack plug; these devices are the perfect solution to get a powerful and good quality audio output from the Raspberry Pi.

Adaption of the telephone pick-up to the stereo speakers holder.

Starting by the Raspberry Pi 3B+ the analog audio output has considerably increased the quality due to the new versions of the Broadcom SoC and the last generation hardware architecture of these embedded Linux machines.

Before disassembling the amplifier I was not yet sure how to fit it inside of the upcycled telephone but as I disassembled the device I saw the solution immediately.

The Stereo Amplifier

It is worth spending a few words on this kind of cheap Chinese amplifiers. Investigating a while I discovered that regardless of their shape the electronics and the other components are almost the same in all the models.

The stereo amplifier after disassembling: electronics, speakers and rechargeable battery.

The device includes a Li-Ion rechargeable battery, a small board with all the electronics with two temporary switches (the control buttons), and a couple of speakers, always of the same diameter.

The very interesting aspect is that the diameter of these speakers it is just the diameter – and the size – of the original speaker and microphone capsule of the telephone pickup. Problem solved!

After desoldering the speakers from the amplifier cable I have reused the original, four wires pickup cable to extend the connection and keep the aspect of the pickup. At the end of this restyling operation, the pickup has been transformed in a couple of original stereo speakers with the amplifier – including the control buttons – and the battery inside the telephone body.

I faced a small issue to control the amplifier with the Raspberry Pi GPIO. The amplifier board – as most of this kind of devices – includes many features but most of them we are not interested:

1. Power On/Off button

2. Bluetooth connection: in this case, we don't need to control the amplifier remotely

3. MP3 player reading data from a Micro SD card

4. Analog audio-in: this is what is needed to play the Raspberry Pi audio output

5. Volume control through two buttons

The power button needs to be pressed for about five seconds to take effect, while the other controls have not any delay.

Also when the amplifier is powered with the audio-in 3.5mm Jack starts in the Bluetooth mode. The last feature is that the volume setting is persistent: when the board is powered-on the volume level is set to the last value at the last shut-down.

Based on the amplifier characteristics, verified experimentally, the Raspberry Pi needs to control two buttons: the power button and the playing mode.

When a temporary switch is pressed it closes a circuit; this means that a simple GPIO logic status High/Low on a GPIO pin is not sufficient to generate any effect on the button.

To simulate the button-press event I used a 2N2222 NPN transistor controlled by a GPIO pin acting as a relay on the button circuit.

After the amplifier board is closed inside the telephone the two controls can only be managed by the Raspberry Pi through the circuit.

The circuit – and the software – dedicated to controlling the amplifier has been designed to work with a specific model. Planning to adopt the same solution with a similar portable amplifier you should investigate how the board works; different models can have small differences in the kind of buttons, functionalities, and delay needed to activate the functions.

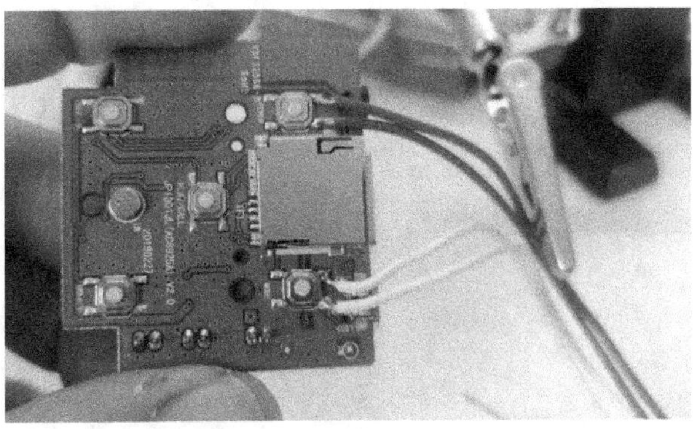

The amplifier board with the two buttons controlled by the Raspberry Pi.

3.4 The Rotary Dialler and the Pickup Switch

This was the most difficult part of the entire project to control digitally.

The dialler is an electro-mechanic device used for numbers composition. When the user moves a hole corresponding to the desired number, the contact is open as the wheel rotates clockwise; rotating the dialler wheel a circular spring is charged.

When the user releases the wheel the charged spring rotates the wheel counterclockwise to the stop position. When the wheel completes the returning rotation it generates a series of pulses approximately every 10 milliseconds.

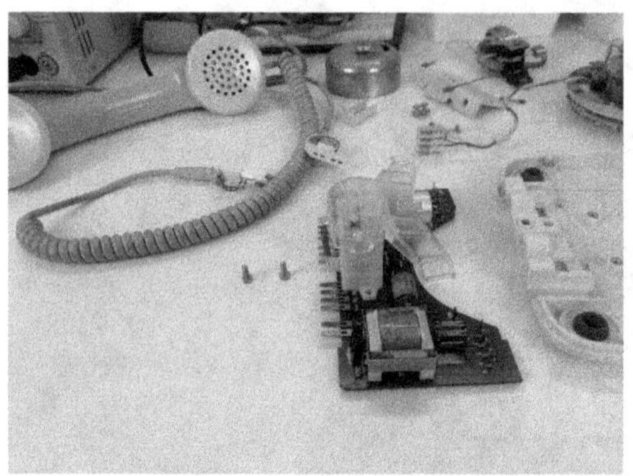

The telephone pickup switch before and after removing the components. It is used as the Pi Rotary activation switch acting like a temporary push button.

The number of pulses corresponds to the dialled number from 1 to 9 while the number 0 is associated to 10 pulses. These pulses are just a contact closed and opened; a GPIO input pin can count the number of pulses generated when a number is dialled.

The behaviour of the rotary dialler can be resumed in two events:

- A first pushbutton remains closed until a dialling sequence has not been completed;

- A second pushbutton generate a number of pulses at regular intervals accordingly to the dialled number.

At least this is what we can detect with two GPIO input pins of the Raspberry Pi.

The dialler device has four wires: two connect the main contact and two correspond to the pulse generator. This part of the circuit is not difficult to make; in fact, the challenging problem has been the development of the software logic to count the pulses without errors.

Another element is part of the user interface in the upcycled telephone: the pickup switch. By the hardware point of view, also this switch can be considered as another pushbutton, detectable by another GPIO pin of the Raspberry Pi.

3.5 The Raspberry Pi Shield

When I figured out the complete scenario of the new features controlled by the Raspberry Pi I thought something was still missing:

- Audio messages and any kind of output controlling the two pushbuttons of the amplifier

- Detect when the user take the pickup switch

- Control the rotary dialler

Indeed, some visual notifications may be helpful for the user to show the different device statuses.

1. When the red LED is on, the telephone can accept commands, corresponding to a numeric sequence.

2. The orange LED flashes when a number is dialled

3. The blue LED is active while the program is running. It is activated when the user takes the phone speakers and stops when the speakers are put down on the pickup.

The Raspberry Pi shield connected to the telephone components on the bench.

To add the signal LEDs I modified and reused two holes already present in this telephone model; their original task was to signal to the user if the incoming call was from an internal room or from the outside line.

The connections from the components of the telephone, as well as the LEDs, were soldered on a small prototype PCB to make it easy to fit Raspberry Pi shield to optimise the space and make it as compact as possible.

3.6 Assembling the Upcycled Device

It was not my intention to make a battery-powered device, at least not when I started the project. The audio amplifier is battery-powered and the battery found space inside the telephone body so I decided to make the whole project battery-operated.

The most compact and efficient solution to power a Raspberry Pi with both a power supply and a battery is adding a *PiJuice* UPS HAT, produced by the PiSupply UK based company.

The Raspberry Pi models 3 or 4 I suggest to use for this project include the onboard WiFi, as well as the RJ45 Ethernet plug. I decided to use the cable connection to make it easy to connect the PiRotary in different places, instead of using the WiFi settings.

Using the network cable or the WiFi is a personal choice that has zero impact on the behaviour of the final project.

The three cables for the amplifier charger, the Raspberry Pi power supply, and the Ethernet cable have been locked on the backside of the telephone with the same plastic clamp originally blocking the phone cable.

Removing the bell ringer and its plastic support from the base of the telephone body I got a good passive cooling system.

The body of the Pi Rotary assembled ready for testing and software development

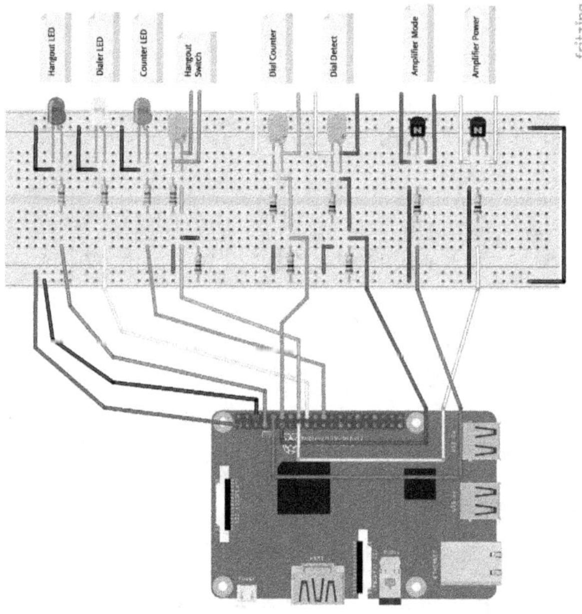

3.7 Circuit and Logic

Developing the Pi Rotary software has been the most complex part of the project.

To reach a full working solution I have done a lot of separate tests to make the single parts working, as well as finding a good approach to harmonise the features running together.

The reason of these problems is due to two factors: the Raspberry Pi Linux architecture is multitasking but we don't know what is the priority assigned by the operating system to these processes.

This has created many issues for the function counting the number of pulses.

Another problem I had to solve was related to the interface. Any input should be sent to the device through the dialler, while the response should be a spoken sentence.

3.8 Software Features

What the Pi Rotary will do and how it will interact with the user? Before starting the development I fixed some must-have characteristics:

- Provide spoken answers and information, in almost any language, possibly customisable

- Play music

- Provide weather report

- Give simple contextual help

- Should be easy to implement new features.

I tried to avoid as much as possible multi-level access to the functions. I think that using only a numeric dialler is annoying and not very efficient dialling more than one number (easy to remember) to get a specific function.

The most basic notifications are provided by the three LEDs informing the user about the current status of the Pi Rotary:

- When the user gets the speaker the pickup switch detects the start of a new session and the blue LED is powered; it stays to On state until the session ends.

- After the session initialisation is completed the red LED changes to On state. At this point, the user can dial a command or require help.

- As the rotary dialler is rotated clockwise, the red LED changes to Off, the system is waiting for the three-numbers command dial.

- When the rotary dialler is released to compose a number, every pulse is signalled by the yellow LED flashing.

- At the end of the sequence if the user has composed a valid command this will be executed.

In order to make any command comfortable to the user interaction – including the session start and end sequences – should be enforced by an audio message.

Tasks Priorities

Before starting programming I had to consider some important aspects related to the priority of the tasks that are executed: some of them can be concurrent, some others should run at the higher priority level possible. The task priority is an essential aspect for the correct performances of the processes.

As a matter of fact, when a sound or voice message is played the Raspberry Pi starts an audio streaming process.

If another event involving the GPIO occurs while playing the sound output lost for a few milliseconds the priority and the output scratches. Another undesired effect is when trying to stream audio output while dialling a number; in this case, the pulses count become unreliable.

The real problem concerns the fact that executing these kinds of tasks concurrently is not an issue for the operating system, but is produced a very unpleasant result. This is the reason that I had to do many experiments to find the best logic – also adopting some compromises – to reach the desired result.

The Control Parameters

To make the entire application fully parametrizable and easy to localise in different languages I have adopted the solution to manage the control parameters externally in two json files: *comments.json* including all the voice messages and *playlist.json* defining the available songs.

```json
{
  "phrases": 9,
  "list": [
    "Pi-Rotary is ready, dial commands when the red light is on. Dial 1 1 1 for help",
    "Closing interactive station.",
    "Starting music player",
    "Play the entire playlist.",
    "Now playing",
    "System booted",
    "Playlist content:",
```

```
      "titles",
      "Wrong command. Please, redial."
    ],
    "helpsentences": 10,
    "help": [
      "Usage information",
      "Wait for the red light before dialling a command",
      "Dial 1 2 3: play all the playlist in order",
      "Dial 1 2 4: list all the playlist titles",
      "Dial 3 2 1: play the next track in the playlist",
      "Dial numbers from 4 0 1 to play the corresponding track in the playlist",
      "Dial 6 6 6: hot reset the Pi Rotary",
      "Dial 9 9 9: cold reset the Pi Rotary",
      "Dial 1 0 0: hear last weather report",
      "Dial 1 1 1: these help notes"
    ],
    "ICAO": "EBBR",
    "airport": "Weather from airport station of Bruxelles. Please wait."
}
```

In the file comments.json shown above, the section *phrases* includes all the messages played by the Pi Rotary in response to the user interaction. The section *help* instead, is played every time the user dials the number *111* to hear the number to dial for the available tasks.

The section *ICAO* – International Civil Aviation Organization airport codes database – should be configured to retrieve the weather report (updated every 15 minutes) of the desired airport. The full list of the ICAO airports can be found at https://www.world-airport-codes.com/

Below, an example of the music configuration file *playlist.json*

```
{
    "tracks": 20,
    "folder": "/home/pi/Music/",
    "files": [
      "001",
      "002",
      "003",
      "004",
```

```
        "005",
        "006",
        "007",
        "008",
        "009",
        "010",
        "011",
        "012",
        "013",
        "014",
        "015",
        "016",
        "017",
        "018",
        "019",
        "020" ],
  "songs": [
        "Precious illusions",
        "Hang on to me tonight",
        "Voyager",
        "Chiquitita",
        "Elephant gun",
        "Suzanne",
        "Tired of sleeping",
        "The Wall",
        "Is there any way out of this dream?",
        "It's all over now, baby blue",
        "The wall",
        "Heroes",
        "Mother",
        "The boxer",
        "Tonight",
        "One of these days",
        "Knockin' on Heaven's door",
        "Missis Robinson",
        "Little bird",
        "Angel in my heart" ]
}
```

Note that the parameter *folder* defines where the mp3 files are saved. This makes it possible to put the track files on an external memory making the playlist upgradable. The full software and component files of Pi Rotary are available under Open Source LGPL 3.0 license on the GitHub repository.

Python 3.x

This an important aspect to take care of: Python 2.7 is no longer developed nor maintained and it is a good practice – especially when developing a new application – to work with Python 3 that is the new official long term Python version. Unfortunately, this change is not always easy to manage; as a matter of fact, the syntax of the new Python version is different and when a library still does not support the new Python 3 some development work is needed to make the porting.

Regardless of this detail, the choice of using Python to manage the skeleton of the whole application is motivated by the fact that this is easy to maintain language and is very portable on different platforms. On the other hand, we should not forget that Python is *interpreted*, that means that in some time-critical operations the performance can be lower than needed. For this reason, some of the features of the Pi Rotary have been implemented using Linux commands and bash scripts. To manage the high-level logic of the entire project instead, Python is a perfect choice.

Controlling the Raspberry Pi GPIO

To control the GPIO of the Raspberry Pi with Python there is not a single official library but there are several ones. The bigger difference of these GPIO Python libraries is the way they manage the hardware In/Out events. In our case, at least to manage the dialler pulses, timing and the software response to the GPIO events is a critical factor so I decided to adopt the *pigpio* library (available on the Pi Rotary GitHub repository). This is a C/C++ library including a well working Python interface, very responsive and according to the tests I carried out the GPIO readings can be synchronous and the percentage of data loss is extremely low.

The library has been compiled from sources to reach the best optimisation on the version Raspbian Linux version used by the Raspberry Pi (tested on Buster distribution too).

```python
import time
import pigpio
import subprocess
import json
PI_HIGH = 1
PI_LOW = 0
# --------------------------------------------------------------------------
# Pin assignment.
# --------------------------------------------------------------------------
pin_hangout_led = 4            # Hangout LED indicator (pin 7)
pin_ampli_mode = 15           # Amplifier mode button (pin 10)
pin_dial_counter = 18          # Count the dialed number (pin 12)
pin_dial_detect = 27           # Detect number dialing (pin 13)
pin_ampli_power = 22           # Amplifier power button (pin 15)
pin_phone_hangout = 23         # Phone hangup/hangout input (pin 16)
pin_dialer_led = 24            # Dialer counter LED (pin 19)
pin_dial_counter_led = 25   # On when the dialer is ready (pin 22)
```

In the first lines of the program after importing the GPIO library the used Raspberry Pi pins are defined as constants.

```python
def set_callbacks():
    '''
    Enable the callback functions associated to the GPIO pins
    and save the callback handlers
    '''
    global pi
    global cb_counter_handler
    global cb_dialer_handler
    global cb_hangout_handler
    cb_hangout_handler = pi.callback(pin_phone_hangout, pigpio.EITHER_EDGE, hangout)
    cb_dialer_handler = pi.callback(pin_dial_detect, pigpio.EITHER_EDGE, dial_detect)
    cb_counter_handler = pi.callback(pin_dial_counter, pigpio.EITHER_EDGE, pulse_count)

    # LED high when the rotary is accepting numbers
    pi.write(pin_dial_counter_led, PI_HIGH)
```

To manage the synchronised events the time-critical tasks are associated with a software interrupt; called when the application starts, the set_callback() function initialises the interrupts with their respective callback functions. This function is called when the program starts (on power-on) and every time a new sequence is initiated by the user taking the speakers pickup.

When one of the interrupt-driven tasks starts all the interrupts are disabled until the end.

Speech Voice Messages

In some previous projects when I needed the Raspberry Pi talking voice messages I followed a pretty tricky way; using Google translate I sampled the text speech of the desired phrase then I used the saved wav as the message. This approach has some serious inconvenient:

- If many voice messages are used in the program the wav audio files occupy a considerable amount of space.

- It is a time-consuming process and it is difficult to maintains using the wav audio files instead of the bare text sentences.

- In case the program has to be localised the work becomes longer and also more complex to maintain.

Then I discovered *trans*, included in the Pi Rotary GitHub repository as well. Trans is a huge bash shell script, fast and efficient, originally designed for translation but including also the ability to speech real-time the desired sentence using the most popular translation sites (selected automatically by the script) like Google Translate, Bing Translator, Yandex.Translate and others. In this case I ignored the translation capabilities of the script using it for text-to-speech conversion only of the message sentences.

The great advantage of using trans is that simply changing the sentence language or text in the json file and the program immediately starts speaking in the desired language from the over eighty supported ones by the translation platforms. Indeed, Pi Rotary needs an Internet connection to run properly.

The Weather Report

This is another feature for which I decided to use an external application, *weather*. This is nice Linux command with a great advantage – in this case – respect other more sophisticated applications. The weather command can generate a text-only output that is easy to parse in Python to extract the report values (temperature, barometric pressure, etc.). Then, with these values, I create a human-readable string that is sent to trans to be spoken.

```python
def get_weather():
    '''
    Retrieve the weather from the nearest airport. The desired international
    airport weather station ICAO four character code should be set in the
    comments.json file.
    The command speak the weather data returned from the call.
    '''
    global is_playing
    global weather_airport
    global weather_ICAO

    # Enable the amplifier and set the playing flag
    is_playing = True
    ampli_on_off()

    # Announce the weather retrieval
    runCmd([TTS[0], TTS[1], weather_airport])

    # Execute the weather command
    cmd = [WEATHER[0], weather_ICAO]

    proc = subprocess.Popen(cmd,
                            stdout=subprocess.PIPE,
                            stderr=subprocess.PIPE,
                            )
    stdout, stderr = proc.communicate()
    # Divide the weather message in a list of single lines
    # removing the newline characters
    forecast = stdout.splitlines()

    w = 4    # First useful line of the weather forecase
```

```python
    # Say the forecast meaningful strings (starting from 4)
    # Note that forecast is a list of bytes so every text line
    # should be decoded to the corresponding ASCII string
    while w < len(forecast):
        text = forecast[w].decode('ascii')
        runCmd([TTS[0], TTS[1], text])
        w += 1


    # Disabe the amplifier, if it has not yet disabled by the user
    if is_playing is True:
        ampli_on_off()
        is_playing = False
```

Calling External Commands With Python

The possibility to call a Linux command directly from the Python program is a very useful option; using this methodology it is possible to define an application skeleton, easy to develop and maintain, in Python while the low-level features or already existing programs can be called effortlessly.

In Linux, a program (including another Python program), a bash command or a compiled executable are all managed in the same way. From the terminal just write the name of the command and it executes or starts. This feature includes programs that show their own GUI (*Graphical User Interface*).

```python
# -------------------------------------------------------------------------
# External commands and json parameter files
# -------------------------------------------------------------------------
# Text-to-speech command and parameters
# Parameters: -sp = speak, -n = narrator voice (not used)
TTS = [ '/home/pi/smartphone/trans', '-sp' ]


# Mp3 play command and parameters. Volume can be a parameter of the command but in
# this case we only use the bare call to the player. The volume is set globally and is
# used by default.
PLAYER = ['mplayer']


# Cold reset command
```

```python
REBOOT = ['sudo', 'reboot', 'now']
# Weather command
WEATHER = ['weather']
```

Most of the Linux commands needs parameters to run correctly. For example, *mplayer* should be called at least with the name of the file to be played. The block of Python code above shows the definition of the external commands used by the Pi Rotary application. To manage easily the external commands call, as well as passing the requested parameters every one of them has been defined as a list. When a command includes some parameter that is mandatory, like the option *-sp* (speech) of the trans script we can add it in the predefined list.

Note that to run an external command from a Python script it is necessary to import the subprocess library. As a matter of fact, in the same way when we start multiple applications from the Linux desktop, every call to an external program is a new process executed by Linux.

A good example of the external command call is shown in the *tts_message()* function below, used to speech a text string

```python
def tts_message(msg):
    '''
    Prepare che message msg to be played as an audio command
    :param msg: The message code accordingly with the list in the
    json file
    :return: 0 or the tts bash command execution error code
    '''

    # Create the full text message
    tText = text_messages[msg]


    return runCmd([TTS[0], TTS[1], tText])
```

The function get the desired message string retrieved from the messages json file and compose the *runCmd* function call shown below. The command name and the other parameters are passed a parameters, if any, to the function.

```python
def runCmd(cmd, extra_info = False):
    '''

    Execute a subprocess command managing the return value, stdout, stderr
    and the return code (0 or not 0 if error occurred)
    :param cmd: The bash command with the parameters
    :return: 0 or the error returncode
    '''


    proc = subprocess.Popen(cmd,
                            stdout=subprocess.PIPE,
                            stderr=subprocess.PIPE,
                            )
    stdout, stderr = proc.communicate()

    return proc.returncode # , stdout, stderr
```

The runCmd() function – used to launch all the external commands used in the program – creates a new Linux subprocess (that means a process depending by the Python calling the main process) passing the command list. It is important to note that the stdout and stderr Linux output (terminal standard output and standard error) are requested to the new running subprocess to get when needed the response of the subprocess inside the Python program.

The Pi Rotary waiting for dialling a command.

Making a Borg

4.1 Seven of Nine

This project won the Grand Prize PiCasso Challenge by <u>element14.com</u> in 2019 and was exhibited for five months, together with other "digital creatures", made by the author, at the Art-a-Tronic exhibition in Gent (Belgium). Link: <u>https://www.element14.com/community/ community/design-challenges/picasso/blog/2019/03/16/art-a-tronic-episode-1</u>

Repository link: https://github.com/alicemirror/mannequin

The creation of the Borg presented in this chapter is the very first vintage upcycling project I ever made. When I designed this project I was far from imagining that in a few months the vintage upcycling would become my main activity as a maker. When the art exhibition closed, I was already collecting nice vintage objects since a few months in order to to upcycle to give them a new life.

The Borg civilisation is based on a hive or group mind known as the Collective. Each Borg drone is linked to the collective by a sophisticated subspace network that ensures each member is given constant supervision and guidance. The mental energy of the group consciousness can help an injured or damaged drone heal or regenerate damaged body parts or technology. The collective consciousness gives them the ability not only to "share the same thoughts", but also to adapt quickly to new tactics. (<u>https://en.wikipedia.org/wiki/Borg</u>)

The Borg and the author.

When I got a mannequin dated 1959 – created with a very original style, very different from the modern ones we see dressed in the shops' windows – I immediately decided that it will become the main character of the Art-a-Tronic exhibition inspired to the Start Trek saga.

One of the characters of the *Voyager* Star Trek series that I liked more is Seven of Nine, the member of the Borg Collective civilisation that episode after episode returns *almost* human. So, nothing else to say, resistance is futile! And the mannequin started his complex adventure to be assimilated.

Looking at the dates when I published for the first time the upcycling projects presented in this book, you will see that I never followed a crescendo of progressive complexity; I always chose them based on the feeling that those objects were suggesting to me at first sight.

4.2 Materials and Components

While cleaning and restoring the mannequin I figured out what practical changes were feasible to implement motion and other features to convert it to the *Seven of Nine* Borg, represented in the final phase of her humanisation.

Excluding the shoulders and wrists, the other articulations of the mannequin are blocked but the entire body is divided into two parts: designing the right mechanics it is possible to rotate the torso. The interior of the body and the head are empty: this means a lot of space to host the new components.

Basically, I designed the Borg architecture around a Raspberry Pi and an Arduino UNO; the microcontroller to manage the movement and the analog inputs, while the Linux embedded represents the brain that controls the behaviour of the animatronic simulating a certain level of consciousness.

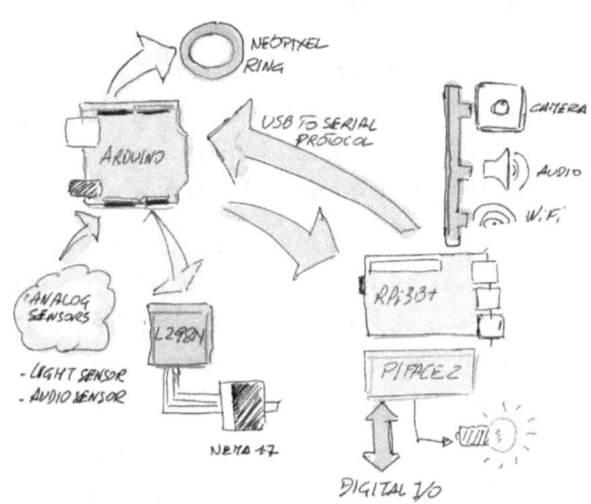

The first draft of the Borg architecture.

Some of the components used for the project.

Project Functional Blocks

After depicting the scenario of the global design I started building single parts to experiment with the ideas. I think this is a good approach for every complex project; following this path it is possible to exploit bugs and function issues, at a single functional block level working in a more comfortable way when the parts are assembled together.

In many cases, I found this approach a winning solution saving a lot of time. It is more complex to identify an issue growing the design as a single structure, while when the project is split in functional blocks things are easier. By the contrary, there is an aspect we should take care and be very cautious: the functional blocks compatibility.

Without considering the parts compatibility and how they will connect together as the very first step of the making process we the risk that we discover at the end some big difficulty to assembly the functional blocks. There is a real case I had to solve in the past that still warn me every time I follow the modular approach in complex projects.

Working on the mannequin

A couple of years ago, wanting to make a cardboard project with lights and motion I decided to use micro servos and some Neopixel LEDs. There were not critical features and I estimated that an Arduino UNO was more than sufficient to manage the few extra components I planned to use. First I developed the software to generate the desired light sequence and everything worked fine; then, while I was 3D printing the case of the lights, I developed the remaining part of the software to control four micro servos.

Also, this second test program worked fine so I continued with the rest of the project: laser cutting the cardboard parts, assembling the lights and after painting and putting all together I wired the animatronic components to the Arduino UNO. In the final sketch, I used both the Adafruit Neopixel Arduino Library and the Arduino Servo Library but nothing worked.

After spending a considerable amount of time to find the reason for the issue I discovered that the two libraries are incompatible. Excluding developing a newly dedicated library this was an issue without a solution.

The Three Steps to Follow When Making Complex Projects

Facing challenging and complex projects, I strongly suggest dividing the project into separate specialised blocks, especially when planning to use different kinds of microcontrollers or embedded devices. According to my personal experience, I suggest to follow these three main steps:

1. After defining the blocks of the project the first task is checking the compatibility of the blocks, as well as for deciding the kind of communication protocol when assembling the parts.

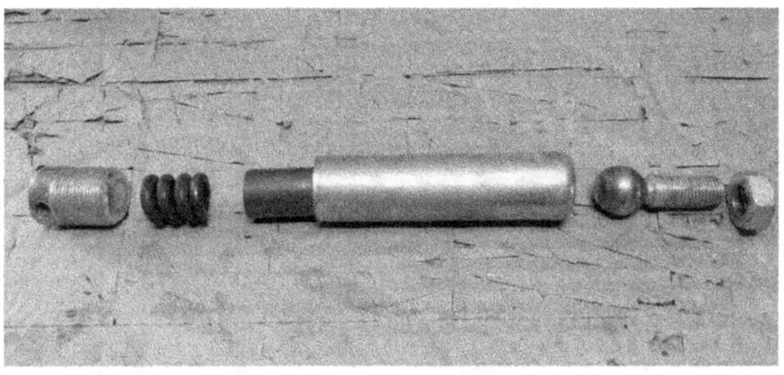

Restoration of the pole supporting the torso of the mannequin.

2. Develop every part on the bench and carefully test it before trying to assemble the entire project. This will help save a lot of time when studying the wiring and connection of the project modules; the approach, in my opinion, is essential when working with an object that should be altered as less as possible, like when upcycling a vintage device.

3. Test the connection of all the parts on the bench before the final assembly. This can help visualise better the scenario, check the blocks working together and find the best solution for the wiring.

Indeed, you should also consider the exceptions; sometimes it is more difficult to test the components out-of-the-box than putting them in-place. In these cases, I adopt what seems an easier solution.

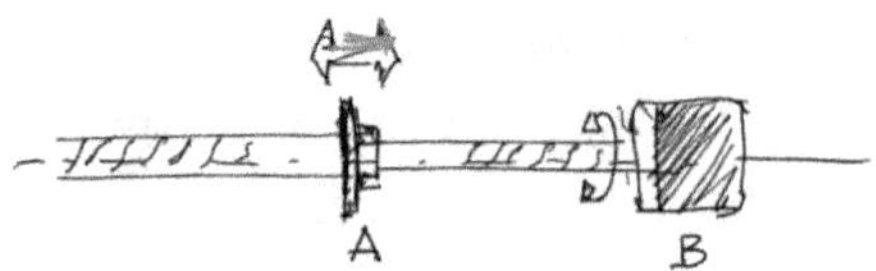

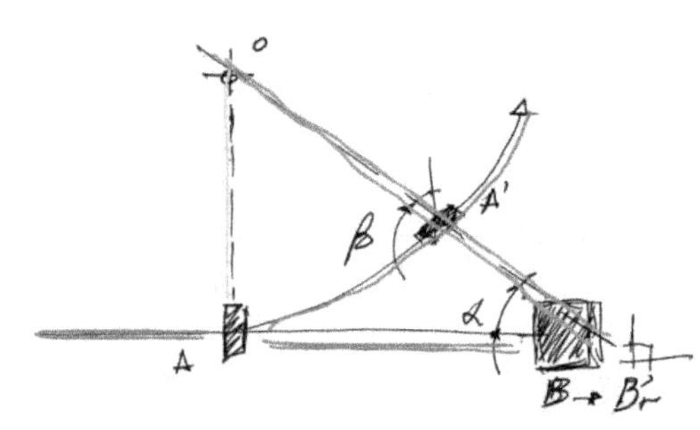

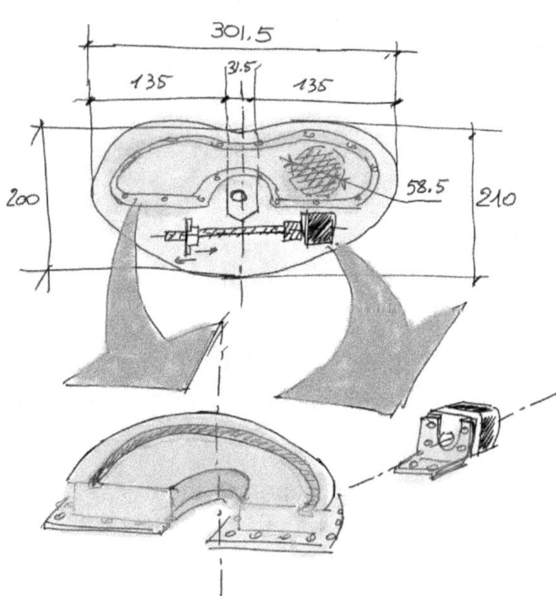

In the project of this chapter, I had to manage two different levels of modular integration; two main modules refer to the Arduino UNO and the Raspberry Pi 3B+. They connects through the USB-Serial cable allowing also programming the Arduino with the Raspberry Pi. The second level of modularity is related to the different software layers working together on the Raspberry Pi.

4.3 Designing the Motion

The mannequin has five moveable nodes built for totally different use: the shoulders articulation to remove the entire arms when dressing, the wrists to remove the hands for the same reason and the torso that can be removed from the base making it more transportable.

I excluded the shoulders and the wrists because to move these articulations the work is too complex, with serious risks to damage the integrity of the original parts. Then, I focused the attention on the torso rotation; the rotation of the body has been sufficient to give to the Borg the scenic effect I desired including that partial rigidity of the movements commonly associated to the androids.

Mechanics

The first mechanic design for the torso rotation was based on a stepper motor with a threaded bar applying positive or negative traction.

I bought the components and tried to see how to design the parts to make the move but then I realised there were two issues: the mechanism was too complex and the size of the *Nema17* stepper motor required too much space between the top and the bottom parts of the mannequin.

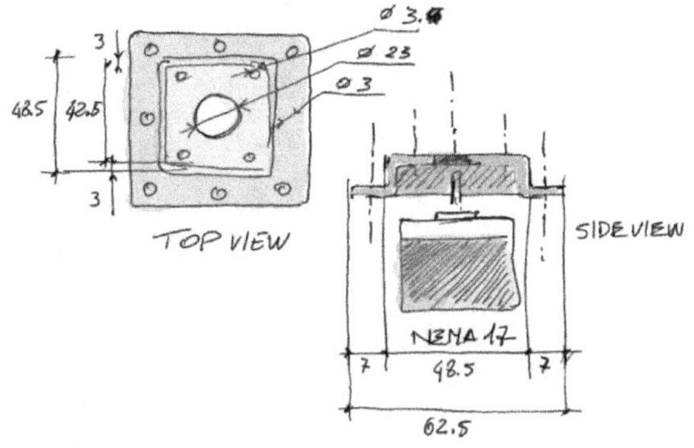

Quoted design of the stepper motor support.

Another problem was the weight of the torso. After installing all the parts inside the body I was expecting a weight of some kilograms; which weight may be excessive if the body rotates on a base covering only half of the body. Then I found a more efficient solution and discarded the option of using this kind of horizontal transducer.

3D printing a *Lazy Susan* bearing the torso lies on a more consistent base while the stepper motor can be inserted in a square hole beside the bearing and connected to it through a tooth-belt. This solution definitely convinced me and I proceeded to put it in place, increasing the distance between the base and the mannequin torso of less than 4 cm.

After making a square hole in the leftmost side of the base I designed with Fusion 360 the stepper support so that the motor body can fit inside the right leg while the only visible part is the 20 teeth pulley.

The flat bearing is made of two large round plates, one screwed to the base and the other to the torso. To keep this custom bearing centred along the rotation axis of the mannequin I reused the pole support blocked in the vertical position.

Lazy Susan bearings are used in low-speed applications to rotate a tray, cabinet, table, or display unit. One side of the bearing attaches to a base. The other side attaches to the rotating platform. If the base is fixed, Lazy Susan bearings allow the tray, cabinet, table, or display unit to rotate a full 360 degrees. (https://en.wiktionary.org/wiki/lazy_Susan)

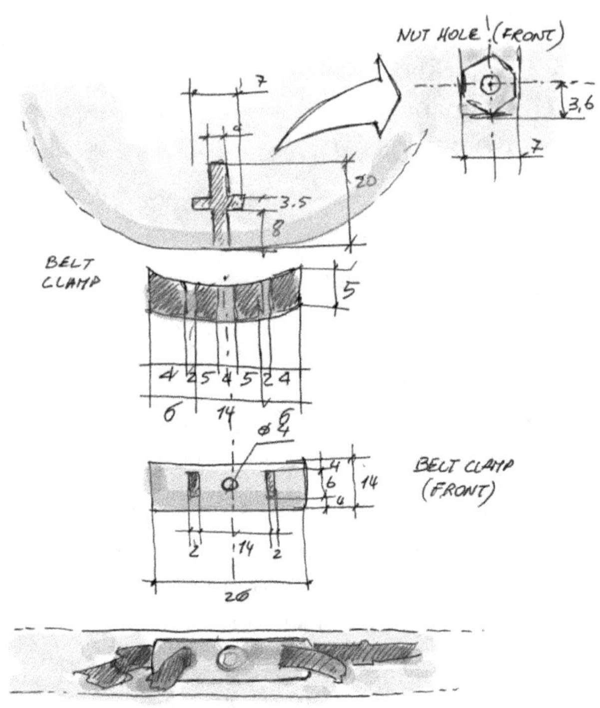

The custom clamp design to keep the tooth-belt in place on the Lazy Susan bearing.

For the iron spheres to smooth the rotating movement between the two halves of the flat bearing I used 3 mm diameter bicycle wheel spheres, bought as spare parts on Amazon.

After both parts were in place I fixed the tooth belt to the bearing driven by the stepper controlled by the Arduino UNO through an L298 motor controller board.

Last-minute update: I found a missing part — my mistake – when the mechanism was in place; I added a small end-stop switch to find the point zero of the torso every time the system is powered on. Also, the switch is controller by a digital GPIO pin of the Arduino.

The torso does not make a full rotation, so the tooth-belt has been tensioned and fixed on the upper part of the flat bearing (the rotating half). With this mechanics, the top body of the mannequin can rotate about 120 Deg in both directions.

In the page below, from top-left to bottom-right the image sequence illustrates the assembly of the torso rotation mechanism as described in this paragraph.

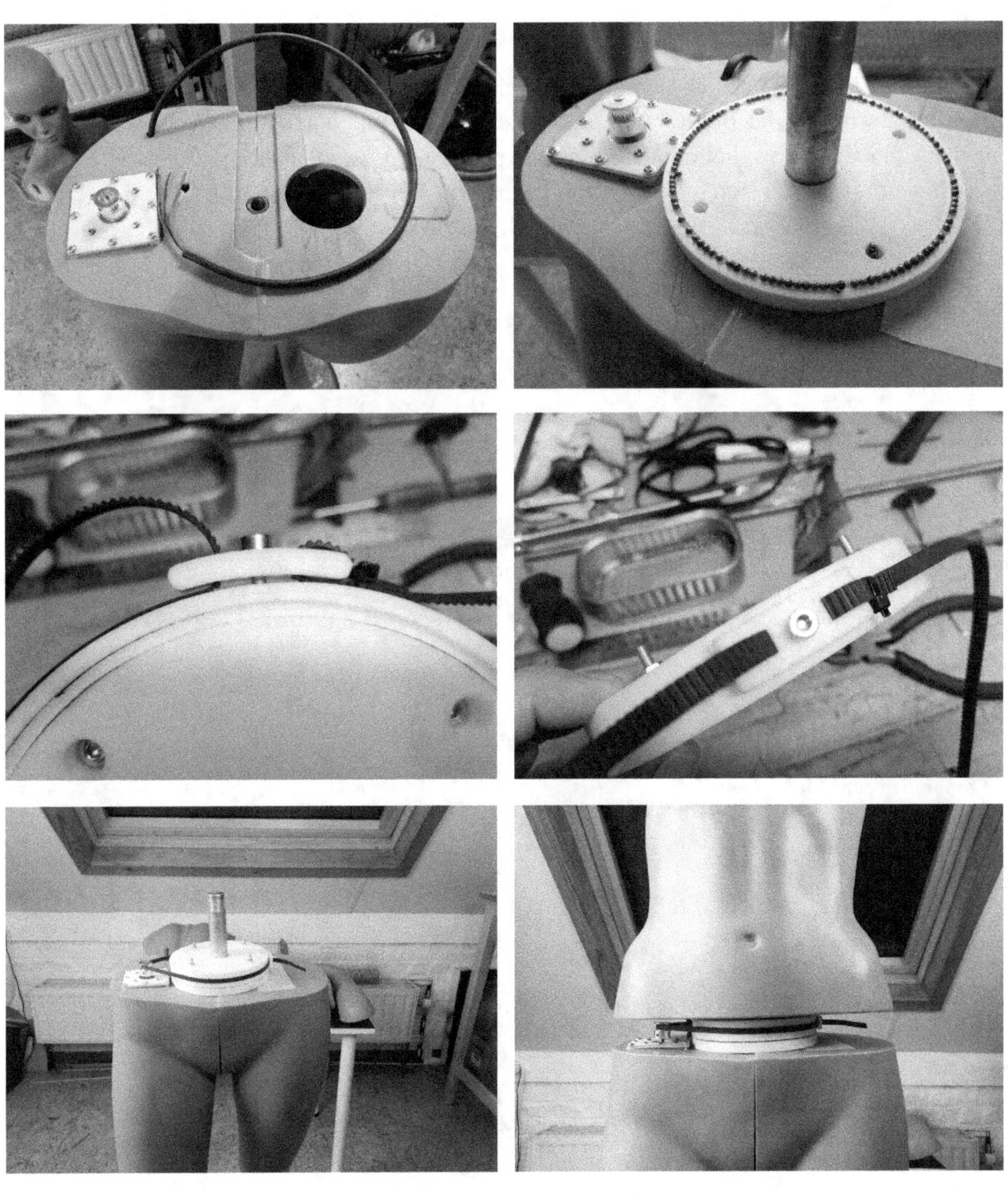

Software

The Arduino UNO sketch includes several parts, to control the torso rotation as well as analog inputs and some other functions. I coded different header files to keep clear the constants and structures that control every feature. The *motor.h* header defines the constants and parameters of the sketch functions controlling the movement.

```
typedef struct StepProfile {
  int torsoSpeed;
  int rotAngle;
  int lastAnglePos;
 };


//! Number of steps per output rotation.
//! Ref.: Nema 17 1.8 DEG/Step
#define STEPS_PER_REVOLUTION 200
//! Demultiplying factor of the large rotating base. According with
//! the two pulleys diameters the reduction factor is 170:14
//! To make a full rotation of the base are needed about 12 stepper
//! pulley rotations.
#define ANGLE_DEMULTIPLIER 12


//! Stepper predefined speed
#define SPEED_LOW 30
//! Stepper predefined speed
#define SPEED_MED 35
//! Stepper predefined speed
#define SPEED_HIGH 45
//! Search zero stepper end point speed
#define SPEED_ZERO 20


//! Increment in angles when searching the endstop point
//! corresponding to the leftmost position
#define SEARCH_ZERO_STEPS -1


//! Max angle in both sides respect to the middel torso position
#define MAX_ANGLE 40
#define MIN_ANGLE 0
```

To make it easy positioning the torso – the direction the Borg is seeing – the rotation is not calculated in steps but the steps are converted in positive or negative rotation angles. increase the performance of the program I must know the virtual number of steps of the rotating bearing. According to the two diameters of the connected parts, I got a reduction factor of 170:14; a full rotation of the base bearing needs 12 full stepper axis rotations.

To emulate different kinds of rotation of the bodyI defined four speeds: SPEED_LOW, SPEED_MED, SPEED_HIGH, SPEED_ZERO. The zero value corresponds to the slow-motion used when approaching the end-stop switch at boot, as well as when the character should change its sight direction very slow.

The microswitch position corresponds to the extreme position of one side rotation and is the initial point reached when the Arduino UNO is powered on. Immediately after the identification of the zero-point, the torso rotates to the absolute mid-position, corresponding to the middle angle of the body. From that point, every rotation is expressed in positive or negative degrees converted in steps.

```
void setTorsoZero() {s
  // Initialize the parameters for zero search
  torsoControl.rotAngle = 0;
  torsoControl.lastAnglePos = 0;
  torsoControl.torsoSpeed = SPEED_ZERO;

  // Search loop
  while(checkEndStop() == false) {
    torsoControl.rotAngle += SEARCH_ZERO_STEPS;
    moveTorso();
  } // Search loop
  torsoControl.lastAnglePos = MIN_ANGLE;
  torsoControl.torsoSpeed = SPEED_LOW;
  torsoControl.rotAngle = MAX_ANGLE;
  moveTorso();
  torsoControl.torsoSpeed = SPEED_LOW;
  torsoControl.rotAngle = MIN_ANGLE;
  moveTorso();
  torsoControl.torsoSpeed = SPEED_LOW;
  torsoControl.rotAngle = MAX_ANGLE / 2;
  moveTorso();
}
```

4.4 The Other Motion-related Components

The choice behind the idea of controlling the motion with an Arduino and the Borg emulation effects with a Raspberry Pi is to make the torso rotation an autonomous closed system, reacting to some environment interactions. The stepper moves the torso as a direct response of the sounds the Borg detects from the environment and occasionally in certain conditions activates a small red laser pointer focused to the sight direction of the body.

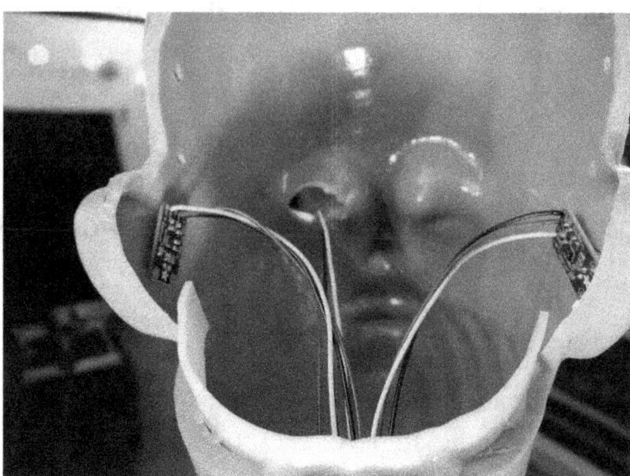

The two electret microphones in correspondence of the hears to detect sound from opposite directions.

Torso Rotation Feedback

To make the torso rotating to "observe" in the direction of a sound I installed two *electret microphones* in correspondence of the ears, each pointing to the opposite direction.

The amount of sound that reaches one of the two sensors compared to the other is directly related to the angle of the sound source compared to the mid-point of the two sensors. By evaluating the difference of the two samples coming from the left and right ear it is possible to calculate the angle of the sound source respect the current position of the torso and rotate it accordingly.

To make these calculations I made a simplified version of the algorithm described in the article *"Acoustic Source Localization and Beamforming"* by Joe C. Chen, Kung Yao, and Ralph E. Hudson from UCLA, California (EURASIP Journal on Applied Signal Processing 2003:4, 359–370.

Below the source of the test algorithm with the calculation of the sound level on the left and right sides.

```
peakToPeak[0] = 0;
peakToPeak[1] = 0;
signalMax[0] = 0;
```

```
signalMax[1] = 0;
signalMin[0] = MAX_SIGNAL;
signalMin[1] = MAX_SIGNAL;

 // collect data for 50 mS from both ears
 while ( (millis() - startMillis) < sampleWindow ) {
   // Check left sample
     sample[EAR_LEFT] = analogRead(A0);
     if (sample[EAR_LEFT] < MAX_SIGNAL) {
        if (sample[EAR_LEFT] > signalMax[EAR_LEFT]) {
           signalMax[EAR_LEFT] = sample[EAR_LEFT];
        } else if (sample[EAR_LEFT] < signalMin[EAR_LEFT]) {
           signalMin[EAR_LEFT] = sample[EAR_LEFT];
        }
     }
 }

delay(50);

 while ( (millis() - startMillis) < sampleWindow ) {
   // Check right sample
     sample[EAR_RIGHT] = analogRead(A1);
     if (sample[EAR_RIGHT] < MAX_SIGNAL) {
        if (sample[EAR_RIGHT] > signalMax[EAR_RIGHT]) {
           signalMax[EAR_RIGHT] = sample[EAR_RIGHT];
        } else if (sample[EAR_RIGHT] < signalMin[EAR_RIGHT]) {
           signalMin[EAR_RIGHT] = sample[EAR_RIGHT];
        }
     }
 }

// max - min = peak-peak amplitude
peakToPeak[EAR_LEFT] = signalMax[EAR_LEFT] - signalMin[EAR_LEFT];
peakToPeak[EAR_RIGHT] = signalMax[EAR_RIGHT] - signalMin[EAR_RIGHT];

volts[EAR_LEFT] = double(peakToPeak[EAR_LEFT] * 5.0) / MAX_SIGNAL;
volts[EAR_RIGHT] = double(peakToPeak[EAR_RIGHT] * 5.0) / MAX_SIGNAL;

double diff = abs(volts[EAR_LEFT] - volts[EAR_RIGHT]);
```

```
    Serial << "Max left " << signalMax[EAR_LEFT] << " Min left " << signalMin[EAR_LEFT] <<
endl;
    Serial << "Max right " << signalMax[EAR_RIGHT] << " Min right " << signalMin[EAR_RIGHT]
<< endl;
    Serial << "peakToPeak left " << peakToPeak[EAR_LEFT] << " peakToPeak right " <<
peakToPeak[EAR_RIGHT] << endl;
    Serial << "V left " << volts[EAR_LEFT] << " V right " << volts[EAR_RIGHT] << endl;
    Serial << " V diff " << diff << endl ;
```

The Laser Pointer

For a better Borg character simulation, I also included a laser pointer that will be fixed to the right temple of the head pointing to the Borg direction of sight.

The 3D printed laser case while developing the software.

Also, the laser pointer is controlled by the Arduino UNO to synch autonomously the body rotation – to change the Borg line of sight – depending on the environment sound and the laser effects.

The component only needs a GPIO pin and the two wires for Vcc and GND; it was easy to connect it on the bench for testing, a bit more complex due to the distance of the parts when fit in place. In the sketch there is a dedicated *laser.h* header file hardcoding all the control parameters used by the sketch functions to create several lighting effects.

```
/**
  Laser status structure.
*/
typedef struct LaserStatus {
  int value;            ///< current laser value
  boolean isOn;         ///< Laser status on/off
};


#define LASER_ON 1       ///< Laser is powered on
#define LASER_OFF 0      ///< Laser if powered off
#define LASER_DEFAULT 16   ///< Default laser value
#define LASER_FIRE 255      ///< Laser fire value (also when burst
#define LASER_FIRE_DURATION 1000    ///< Laser fire shot duration (ms)
#define LASER_OFF_BEFORE_FIRE 50     ///< Delay after powering out the laser before firing
#define LASER_BURST_DURATION 50      ///< Duration of a single burst
#define LASER_BURST_PAUSE 25      ///< Duration of a single burst
#define LASER_BURST_LENGHT 3       ///< Number of bursts
#define LASER_LONG_BURST 5        ///< Number of multiple bursts
#define LASER_FADE_DELAY 25        ///< Fade steps delay (ms)
```

The *laser control* section of the Arduino sketch includes a series of functions shown that can be used according to the kind of movement. The laser control pint uses a PWM digital output so it is possible to control also the intensity of the beam, as well as the flashing sequence.

```
/**
  Set the laser state. If the state is set to on, the laser level is
  assigned else the level value has no effect.
*/
void setLaser() {
 if(laser.isOn) {
   analogWrite(LASER_PIN, laser.value);
 } // Laser is on, set the value
 else {
   analogWrite(LASER_PIN, 0);
 } // Laser disabled
}

/**
```

```
   Laser single shot with variable duration

   @param fireDuration The duration of the fire. The function is used
   both by the fireLaser() and burstLaser()
   */
void fireLaser(int fireDuration) {
  // Save the current laser values
  LaserStatus laserBackup;
  laserBackup.value = laser.value;
  laserBackup.isOn = laser.isOn;

  // First, disable the laser
  if(laser.isOn) {
    laser.isOn = LASER_OFF;
    setLaser();
    delay(LASER_OFF_BEFORE_FIRE);
  }
  // Set the fire value then executes the action
  laser.value = LASER_FIRE;
  laser.isOn = LASER_ON;
  setLaser();
  delay(fireDuration);
  // Restore the previous laser status
  laser.value = laserBackup.value;
  laser.isOn = laserBackup.isOn;
  setLaser();
}

//! Execute the single shot
void fireLaser() {
  fireLaser(LASER_FIRE_DURATION);
}

//! Execute a burst sequence
void burstLaser() {
  int j;

  for(j = 0; j < LASER_BURST_LENGHT; j++) {
    fireLaser(LASER_BURST_DURATION);
```

```c
    delay(LASER_BURST_PAUSE);
  }
}

//! Execute multiple bursts
void longBurstLaser() {
  int j;

  for(j = 0; j < LASER_LONG_BURST; j++) {
    burstLaser();
  }
}

//! Fade off the laser from the current value
void laserFadeOff() {
  int j;

  laser.isOn = LASER_ON;

  // Fade off loop
  for(j = laser.value; j >= 0; j--) {
    laser.value = j;
    setLaser();
    delay(LASER_FADE_DELAY);
  }
}

//! Fade on the laser to the current value
void laserFadeOn() {
  int j, value;
  laser.isOn = LASER_ON;
  value = laser.value;
  // Fade off loop
  for(j = 0; j <= value; j++) {
    laser.value = j;
    setLaser();
    delay(LASER_FADE_DELAY);
  }
}
```

Using the *LaserStatus* structure defined in the *laser.h* header the sketch *loop()* function knows in any moment the state of the device.

4.5 Preparing the Brain

All the behavioural simulation of the Seven of Nine Borg by the mannequin is in charge to the Raspberry Pi (in this case I have used a Pi 3B+, but a Raspberry Pi 4B generation may work fine as well). As there are many functional aspects covered by the Raspberry Pi, I developed a different component for every task; the main software architecture has been developed in Python but there are also external commands and some autonomous processes that rung independently, based on Linux commands not necessarily connected to the main Python components.

The Vision System

Every Borg has a special implant in one of its eyes for artificial vision, as well as for sending what it sees to the other members of the Borg Collective.

Also, after Seven of Nine was fully recovered and was human again part of eye implant still remains visible on her face.

To do this, I added a Raspberry Pi Camera V.2 and transformed the left eye of the mannequin.

More details on the 8 Mp Raspberry Pi Camera can be found on the official Raspberry Pi site: https://www.raspberrypi.org/documentation/hardware/camera/

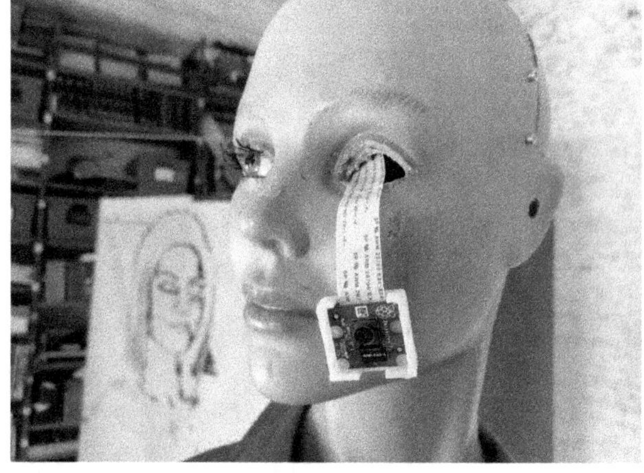

The Pi Camera out of the left eye of the Borg.

The Borg's Voice

The Borg should speak. A considerable part of the work to make the Borg speaking has been covered by the software development but the Raspberry Pi has only audio out 3,5 mm jack; to make her "voice" audible I have included a small, 3W audio amplifier and a small speaker.

The bench set up of the components during testing and software development.

To avoid keeping the speaker inside the head generating distorted sounds I used a smartphone speaker, characterised by the wide range of frequencies and very small size.

Speakers of this kind can be found almost cheap on the Farnell site: https://export.farnell.com/visaton/2941/loudspeaker-mini-oval-8-ohm/dp/1675524

A Pulsating Hearth

When a human is assimilated (resistance is futile!) to the Borg civilisation the person loses his own identity and become a mix of biology and technology components.

Seven of Nine, indeed, always deserved in her deepest being a part of humanity. I decided to represent this fictional-philosophical concept adding a pulsating lamp placed inside the torso visible through the small transparency of the nylon body of the mannequin.

The lamp I found was perfect for the scope: a yellowish 220V AC lamp simulating a flame; To control the digital signals with the Raspberry Pi I have used a *PiFace Digital 2 Pi HAT* (http://www.piface.org.uk/products/piface_digital_2/) The PiFace HAT communicates with the Raspberry Pi using the fast SPI protocol exposing eight open-collector digital pins; two of these pins can be configured to control a relay, also included on the board.

The Raspberry Pi with the PiFace Digital 2 Shield

Unfortunately, the PiFace relays only support up to 30 V; to control the 220V lamp I added a second relay that can support up to 250 V AC. Problem solved with little effort.

Completing the Eye Implant

The eye implant is the last trace that will remain forever on the Seven of Nine's face to remind that also after her full recovery she is still a Borg. This implant not only provides vision capabilities to the Raspberry Pi but also flashes periodically a random, suggestive light sequence.

To create that effect I designed and 3D printed the implant, then I added behind it a ring built with seven high-intensity cold-white LEDs. The lighting sequence is managed by the Raspberry Pi applying several kinds of cyclic sequences using the seven unused pins of the PiFace HAT.

The Next Step

At this point, all the hardware parts have been set up, connected and tested, and the software architecture is clearer.

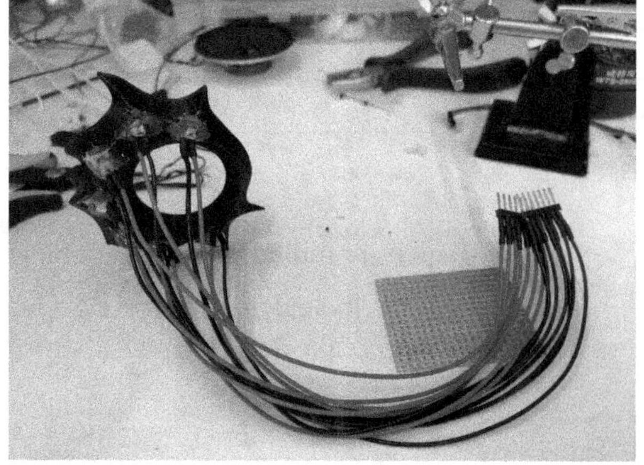

The eye implant with the seven LEDs that will flash from the back.

After completing the assembly of the components, before moving to the software development it is necessary to start wiring and assembling the components inside the body. As a matter of fact, most of the effects should be seen in-place to calibrate correctly the programs and automated scripts to get the desired effect.

From this point, the Mannequin transformation will start for strong change. The second part of the making of this project was an alternation between hard modifications and software development; in many cases, the final solution was the result of these frequent development and feedback. Until the end of the upcycling process.

4.6 Body Modifications and Wiring

With the mechanics for the torso rotation assembled on the base of the body the torso needs modifications to host the new components, power supplies, and wires.

It has been necessary to make accessible both the top of the body (yes, I cut the mannequin head!) and the bottom; The Raspberry Pi should be near to the Pi Camera so the best possible solution is to fit it in the middle of the head, while the Arduino together the 220V AC relay and the L298 stepper motor controller should stay on the base of the torso.

There are lots of wires that should connect the top and the bottom side. I kept inside the power lines and the USB cable to connect the Arduino UNO while the signal wires are outside of the body. For the external wiring, I used a black sheath, another detail contributing to remember the Borg origins of Seven of Nine.

Adapting the Body

The need to cut the torso to install the components inside can't be ignored; after investigating all the possibilities – with the consciousness that there was only one possibility – I have decided to make a square hole to the back bottom of the shoulder. This represented the minor issue: the cut part will be covered by the rectangular piece, invisible when the Borg is dressed.

The real issue was how to fit the Raspberry Pi and the amplifier inside of the head. The only possible solution was to cut the head in a way to preserve the aesthetic of the character and giving easy access to the head inside.

The last changes have been making the holes in correspondence of the ears to place the sound sensors and empty the left eye to insert the camera (with the flat cable connected to the Raspberry Pi) and the eye implant; when put in place, these two parts completely hide the eye hole.

The images in the page below show some of the phases of the body adaption to add the components inside.

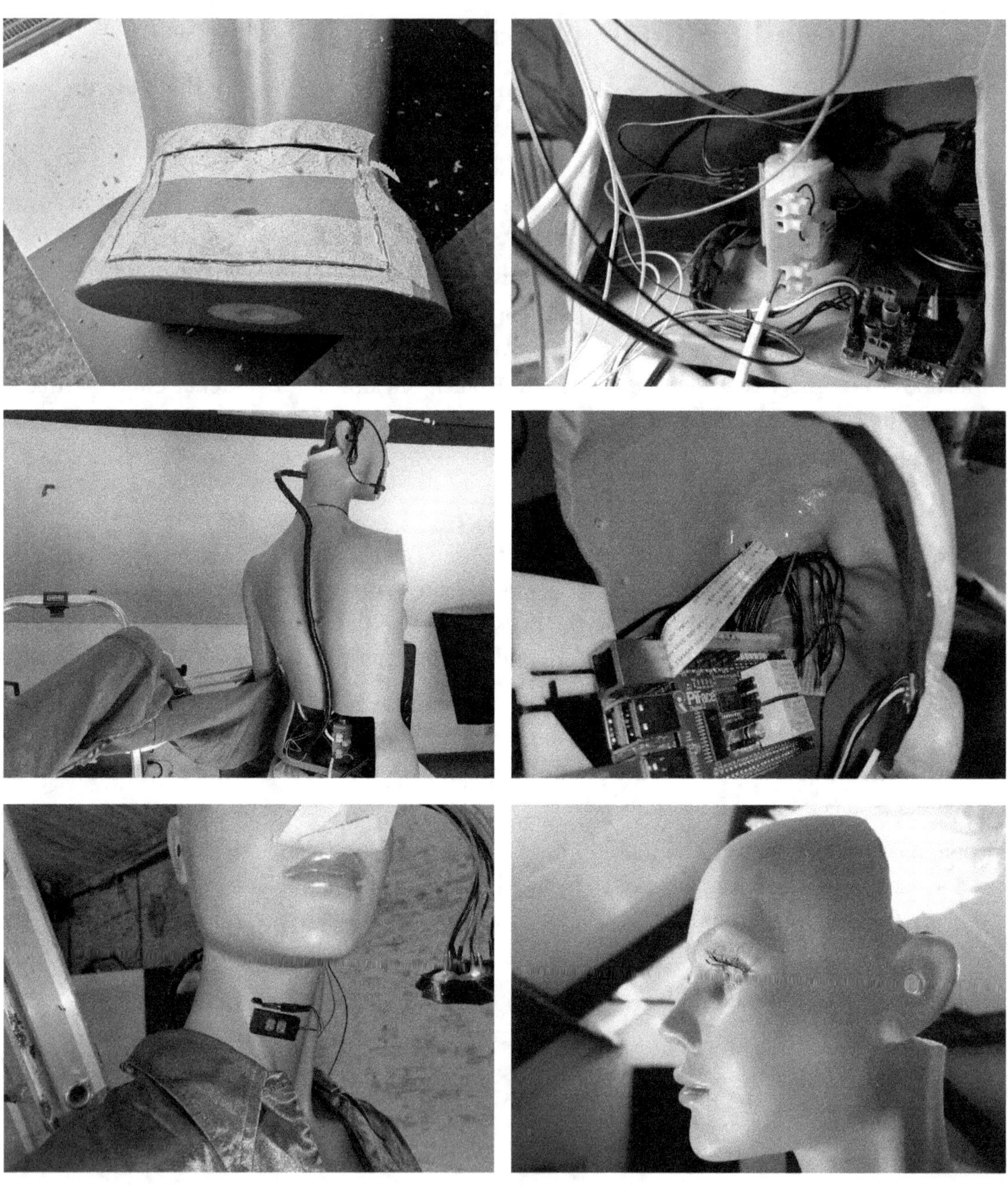

Fine Tuning

The assembly and wiring, as frequently happen has not been linear and easy to do; in many cases, I faced last-minute issues solved inventing some kind of alternative to what I was thinking.

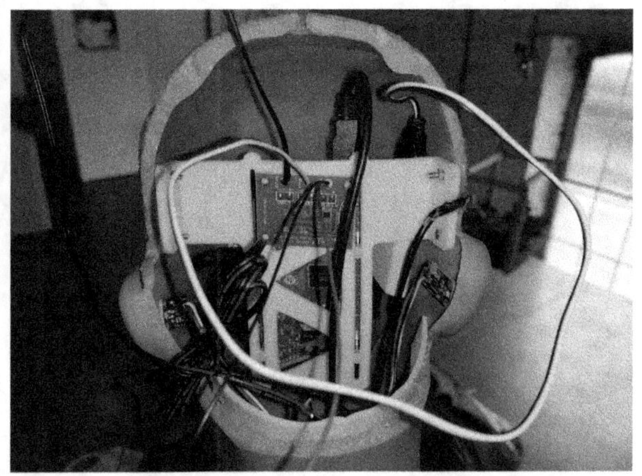

The 3D printed support holding the Raspberry Pi on one side and the audio amplifier to the other.

For example, the problem of keeping the Raspberry Pi in the centre of the head has been solved designing and 3D printing support screwed to the sides of the head.

Another problem that required to remove twice the wires from inside the body was the 220V AC lamp. In my first try I have not considered that this part – kept in place by another custom 3D printed support screwed in the mid of the back – was impossible to fix if all the cables were connected from the top to the bottom of the body.

After placing the lamp and the support I met another issue: due to the reduced space, it was impossible to insert the wires pushing them through the neck hole as I have done before. This issue was solved using a cable gland probe and pulling the cables one by one.

To avoid heating risks and optimise the power distribution I decided to put the power supplies glued internally to the belly; I had to add the power supply for the Raspberry Pi, a 9V DC power supply for the Arduino, a 5V DC for the stepper motor and one for the audio amplifier.

To provide a single 220V power cable to the external I soldered and insulated the 220V AC plug of every power unit to a couple of wires screwed to a small prototype PCB with a terminal block, also connecting the relay powering the 220V flame-like lamp.

Then, the last problem: how to close the cut part of the head after the assembly had been completed? Also in this case I had to 3D print a custom part glued to the neck to which fixe the back of the head part with the possibility to reopen it when needed.

## CHAPTER 5

Radio Magic

5.1 A First Musical Project

This project first appeared on "The Shed" magazine issue number 92, September/October 2020 (https://the-shed.nz/) and has been introduced in the second Project14 workshop "Vintage Upcycling" by https://www.element14.com/community/community/project14/hardwarehacking/blog/2020/06/17/radio-magic-sounds-nice-part-1

Repository link: https://github.com/alicemirror/RadioMagic

Radio Magic is the name of a series of three projects completing the upcycling series of this book. This upcycling of a 1960' Bush Radio names the three projects series; it is a path I started last year to make music with vintage technologies integrated to the most recent hardware and software devices available today.

As already mentioned in this volume, with the upcycling projects I tried to propose ideas, some methodological suggestion and – hopefully – inspiring other makers to hack, change, rebuild and adapt the projects to their vintage devices. Consider this project as a proposal to upcycle an old transistor radio to something new, almost any kind of radio of the same period.

How can an old transistor radio be used to make music?

Electronic music can be created with digital or analogue synthesisers: it is an electronic device able to generate some kinds of a waveform in the audible range (from 20 to 20.000 Hz). There are a lot of functions that can be added to a simple waveform to apply any kinds of effect, chaining together multiple devices or software modules to change the original sound giving accents, modifying decay, duration, attack and much more.

Indeed, this is not the only kind of approach to electronic music; instead of artificially generated sounds, we can sample them. In many modern synthesisers, the instruments are built starting from a real-world sample. A sound sample is the recording of a short sequence of sounds: a musical instrument, a noisy tool, the sound generated by a percussion, or –why not – a vintage radio.

The author and the radio, a *Blue Baby* special edition of the BUSH transistor radio, 1960 circa.

One of the first music synthesisers was the Mellotron is an electro-mechanical musical instrument developed in Birmingham, England, in 1963. The instrument is played pressing its keys, each of which pushes a length of magnetic tape against a capstan, which pulls it across a playback head. Then as the key is released, the tape is retracted by a spring to its initial position. Different portions of the tape can be played to access different sounds. (https://en.wikipedia.org/wiki/Mellotron)

The mid-60' BUSH radio of which I own a Blue Baby limited edition required some upgrade to become a sound generator. The interesting aspect of sampling from a radio is the ability to tune the receiver covering nearby frequencies creating a continuous variation of random sound and noise.

The possibilities offered to create new and original musical instruments with this method are limitless; changing the tuning while sampling we can sample a mix of sounds used as the base to generate an entire set of notes.

5.2 Hacking the Radio Tuner

To hack the tuner to automatically change the radio station I checked how it works inside of the radio.

The radio tuning is controlled by a *variable capacitor*, a widely used component in the radios produced for many decades until the early 70'.

It is not easy operating the right selection rotating the shaft of the variable capacitor. The tuning mechanism has a thin cotton thread connected through a pulley to the manual knob, increase the rotation for more precise identification of the desired band.

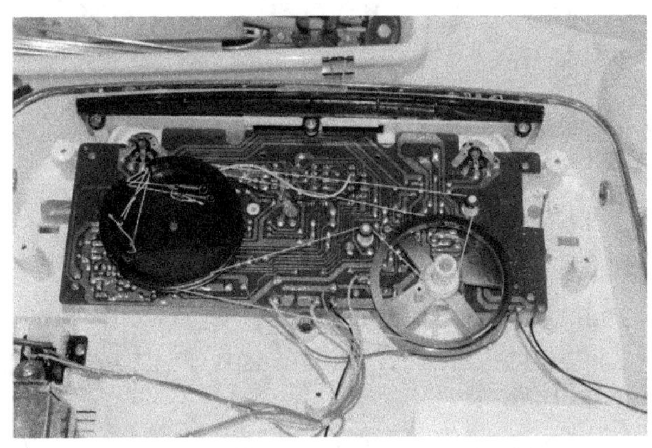

The tuner mechanism: the variable capacitor to the left and the tuner knob to the right.

A variable capacitor is a device whose capacitance may be intentionally changed mechanically or electronically. Variable capacitors are often used in L/C circuits to set the resonance frequency, e.g. to tune a radio (therefore it is sometimes called a tuning capacitor or tuning condenser).

According to the transistor radios technology, the solution described in this project can be easily applied – with some minor adaptions – to a wide range of vintage radios.

The Tuner Mechanism

The variable capacitor has a large pulley driven by the knob pulley through a cotton thread doing a complex path. I wanted to gain direct control to the variable capacitor inverting the functions of the two pulleys.

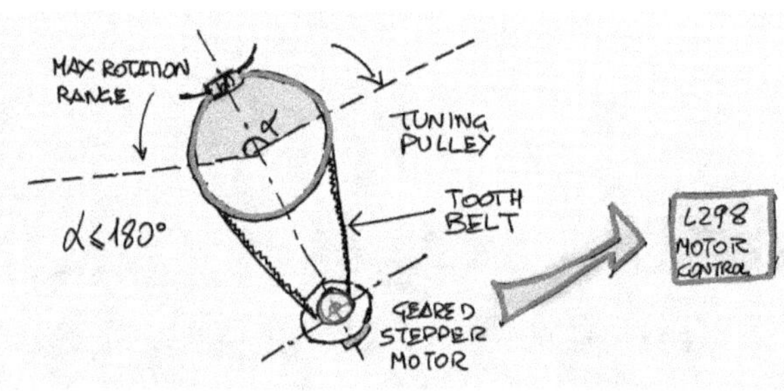

The variable capacitor rotation angle and the optimal position of the stepper motor.

After opening the radio case I verified that rotating the variable capacitor pulley the knob pulley moves without difficulty: this means that at least in theory this operation is feasible.

Moving the tuner pulley requires a considerable precision as the movement range is less than 180 deg.

I excluded a DC motor because the mechanism should be able to make very short increments of the variable capacitor angle of the shaft; for this reason, I decided to use a geared stepper motor 28BYJ-48 (https://opencircuit.shop/Product/28BYJ-48-5V-stepper-motor-4-phase-5-wire), an inexpensive 5V stepper motor.

Due to its reduced dimensions, it is perfect to be added inside of the case of the radio while the reduction gear gives the slow speed and torque needed to move the tuner pulley.

5.3 The New Components

A considerable part of the case is occupied by the back of the big mono speaker of the radio.

To place the stepper motor shaft in-line with the tuner pulley I had to remove the speaker.

To use the radio as a sampling device the only useful output is the audio output, a 3.5 mm jack on top of the radio. Excluding the amplifier to remove the speaker does not impact the project expectations.

After removing the speaker I checked the available space and the thickness of the case. About 2,5 cm were still available on top of the tuner. I planned to insert the stepper motor and an extra pulley inside this space.

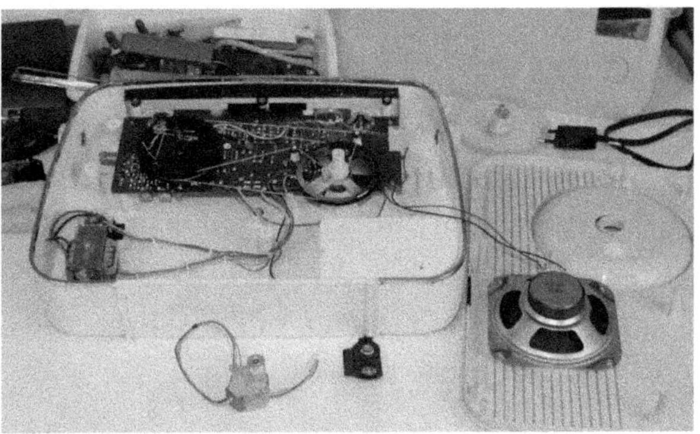

The large speaker on the case top cover has been removed to make space for the stepper motor.

For the movement transmission between the motor and the tuner, I used a 6mm tooth-belt; the stepper motor should be at the same height of the driven pulley for the right movement.

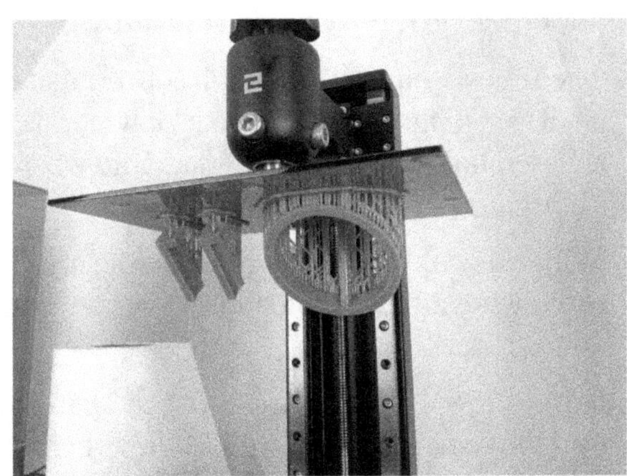

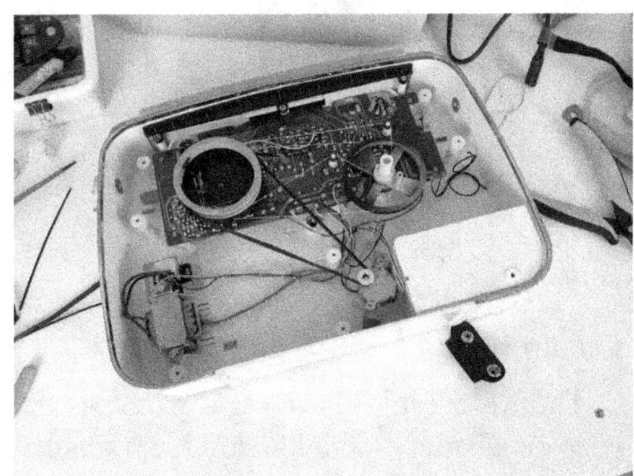

The 3D printed parts (left) and the motor connected through the tooth-belt to the second tuner pulley (right).

To drive the tuner shaft, I had a limitation, preserving the original pulley to drive the tuner knob while the motor changes the position. The solution has been designing with Fusion360 and 3D with the LCD Elegoo Saturn 3d printer (https://www.elegoo.com/collections/frontpage/products/elegoo-saturn-msla-4k-monochrome-lcd-3d-printer).

I had to take care of the right dimensions as the 12 teeth of the stepper motor should be at the same height as the tuner pulley, and the added parts should not be higher than 1.5 cm.

To support the stepper motor, I used two separate supports that can be regulated to give the right tension to the tooth-belt.

The new components assembled and connected to the RJ45 plug on the right side of the radio.

Thanks to a small square hole connecting the battery holder on the back to the radio circuit, it was possible to replace the battery holder with the L298 stepper controller board.

To keep the almost intact the device exterior, I faced the problem of how to connect the six wires needed to control the motor: four for the stepper and two for powering the L298 controller board.

The tiniest solution I found has been using an RJ45 plug: I had to make only a small squared hole on one side of the radio where I hot-glued an Ethernet plug.

With this solution, a single Ethernet patch cable was sufficient to connect the radio to the control board.

The RJ45 cables have eight wires; as the radio needs 9V power (I removed the battery holder for a battery model no longer available), I used the remaining two wires of the Ethernet cable to power the radio itself.

5.4 The Control Board

After setting the mechanics and testing the connection and motor working I started working to the Radio Magic control board. The task of this board is giving visual feedback to the user moving the tuner with a knob and program it to start moving the tuner between a range selected by the user.

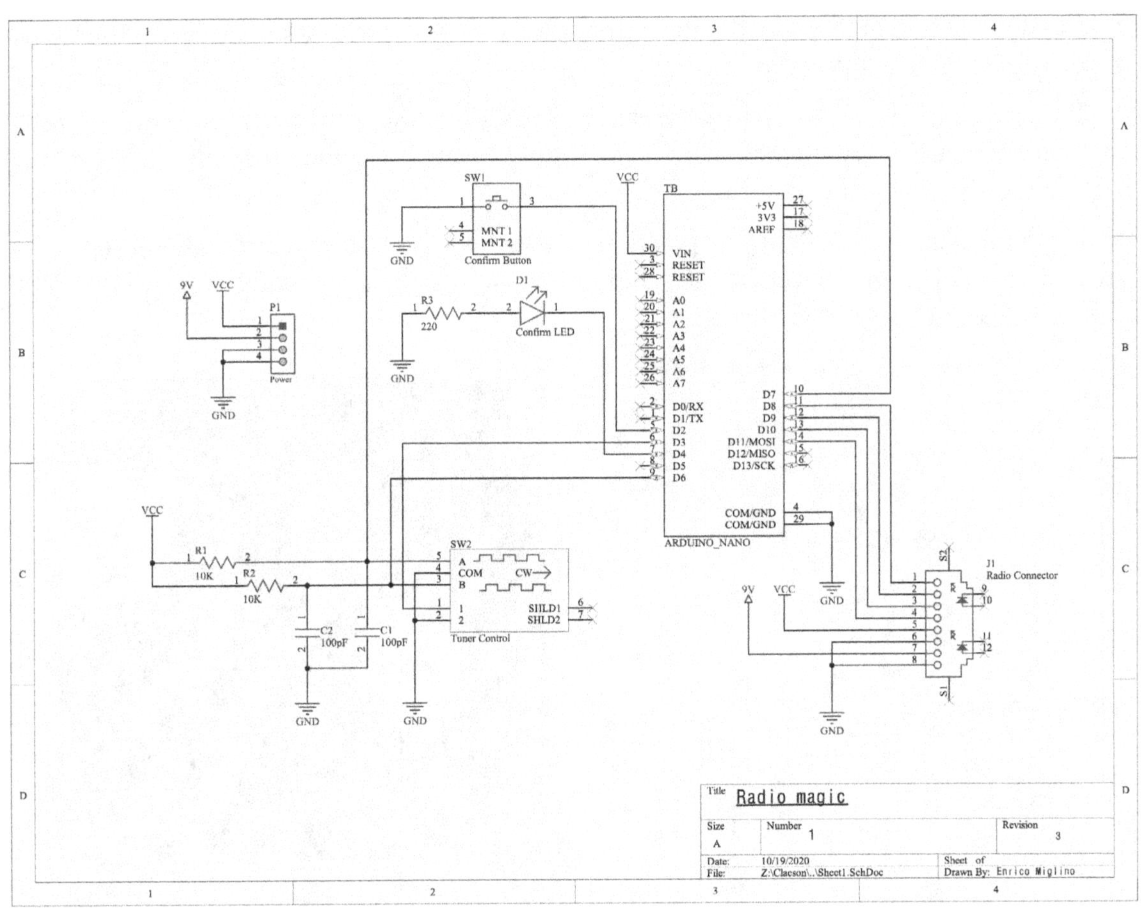

Schematics of the Radio Magic control board. The circuit includes an Arduino Nano that control the logic of the programmable tuner. Created with *Altium Designer*.

As shown in the schematics, the core part of the board is an Arduino Nano controlling the logic of the tuner. The motor movement and direction are controlled by the Arduino, through a rotary encoder.

Another feature of the board is the ability to program the tuner setting; when the user positions the tuner on the desired frequency, pressing the pushbutton of the rotary encoder a green LED signals the acquired position.

Then the user should rotate the tuner again (no matter the direction) and press the rotary encoder pushbutton another time.

Programming is set and the motor starts rotating the tuner continuously in both directions until the rotary encoder knob is not rotated again. A second pushbutton can be used to temporary stop/start the rotation.

As the feedback of the current position of the tuner is shown accordingly on the radio gauge of the knob – now driven by the tuner – it was not necessary to add a stop switch to the extreme sides of the rotation range.

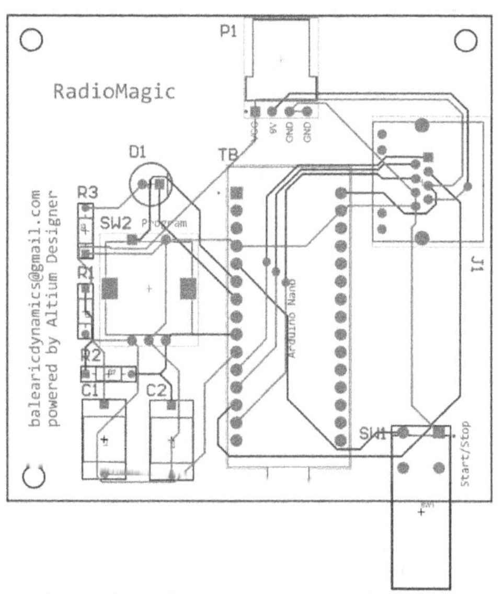

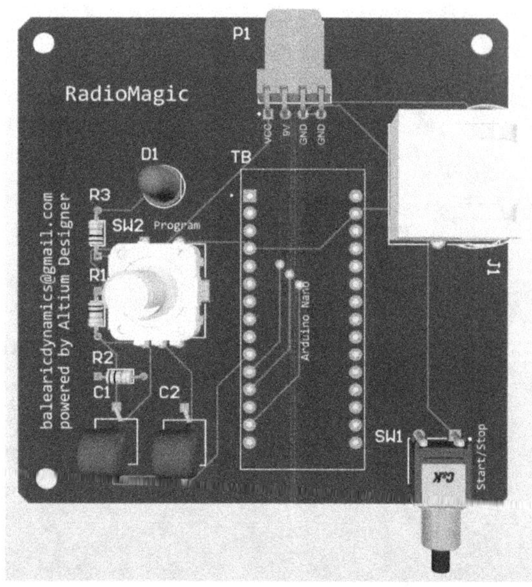

The control board routed PCB (left) and a 3D simulation of the board (right). Created with *Altium Designer*.

The assembled PCB (left) and the control board connected to the radio during the software development (right)

5.5 The Arduino Sketch

Managing the features seems a simple task but getting the system reactive and fast required some software solutions that are worth to see in detail. The architecture of the software manages asynchronously three components: the notification LED, the stepper motor and the rotary encoder.

The program logic works as a state machine, where every state changes the behaviour of the components. For example, the rotary encoder will disable the programmed rotation when it is moved, while the LED blink different according to the state of the program without blocking the main loop activity.

The snapshot of the program is defined in the RadioStepper structure. It is updated every loop() cycle.

```
/**
 * The RadioStepper structure contains the status of
 * all the parameters controlling the behavior of the radio
 */
struct RadioStepper {
  /**
   * The starting position has been selected
   *
```

```
 * This happens when the user press for the first
 * time the rotary encoder button. From that point,
 * the number of effective steps is counted until
 * the button is not pressed for the second time.
 */
bool isSelected = false;

/**
 * When the button has been pressed for the second time, the
 * programmed status indicates that the system is ready to
 * loop the tuner.
 */
bool isProgrammed = false;
//! Status enabled when the tuner is looping
bool isLooping = false;
//! Current relative tuner position inside a loop
int tunerPosition = 0;
//! Looping direction. It is inverted when one of the two limits
//! is reached
int loopDirection = 0;

/**
 * Steps units expressed in number of rotary pulses
 *
 * The units are added algebraically to the counter until
 * the rotary encoder button is not pressed for the second
 * time. At this point the controller is programmed to execute
 * a loop.
 */
int loopSteps = 0;
//! Current rotary encoder position
int16_t encValue = 0;

//! Current LED non-stop blinking frequency
//! It is different when looping is stopped by the stepper is
//! programmed
int blinkLEDFrequency;
//! LED status, inverted during the non-blocking blinking mechanism
boolean isLEDOn = false;
```

```
//! Starting millis to calculate the period for LED blinking in the
//! non-blocking function
unsigned long millisCounter;
};
```

LED Activity

The LED communicates to the user the tuner programming status:

LED off: no programmed motion is active

Fixed light: the tuner starting point is loaded

Blink at 10 Hz frequency: the tuner is moving in the programmed range

Blink at 1 Hz frequency: tuner is programmed but in standby mode

The LED status is updated every loop() cycle. The LED blinks depending on the milliseconds value and the state of the program at that moment.

```
/**
 * Blink the signal LED once, inverting the status of the LED. This function should
 * be used during uninterruptable LED blinking.
 *
 * The LED status is changed only if the right frequency time has passed else the function
 * do nothing.
 */
void blinkLEDOnce() {
  // Check if it is blink time
  if( ((millis() - radioStepper.millisCounter) >= radioStepper.blinkLEDFrequency) &&
radioStepper.isProgrammed) {
    // Invert the status of the LED
    if(radioStepper.isLEDOn) {
      digitalWrite(PROG_LED, LOW);
      radioStepper.isLEDOn = false;
    }
    else {
      digitalWrite(PROG_LED, HIGH);
      radioStepper.isLEDOn = true;
    }
    // Update the counter
    radioStepper.millisCounter = millis();
```

```cpp
  }
}

/**
 * Blink the signal LED for a specified period (ms). If the period duration is
 * less than the frequency needed to blink twice, the function do nothing.
 *
 * \param period The blink duration in ms
 */
void blinkLEDPeriod(int period) {
  // Check that the period is at least four times the blink frequency
  if(period / 2 >= LED_FREQ * 2) {
    //! The number of blinks (On/Off) of the LED
    int stepBlink = period / LED_FREQ;
    //! Blink loop
    int j;
    boolean isOn = true;

#ifdef DEBUG
    Serial << "blinkLEDPeriod(" << period << ") stepBlink " << stepBlink <<
            " Frequency " << LED_FREQ << endl;
#endif

    // Loop for the needed period
    for(j = 0; j < stepBlink; j++) {
      // Invert the last LED status and set the LED
      if(isOn) {
        digitalWrite(PROG_LED, HIGH);
        isOn = false;
      }
      else {
        digitalWrite(PROG_LED, LOW);
        isOn = true;
      }
      delay(LED_FREQ);
#ifdef DEBUG
      Serial << " " << isOn;
#endif
    }
```

```
    // Reset the LED to off
    digitalWrite(PROG_LED, LOW);
#ifdef DEBUG
    Serial << endl << " END." << endl;
#endif
  }
}
```

The led blinking is controlled through two functions shown above: *blinkLEDPeriod()* that blinks the LED for a predefined period, and *blinkLEDOnce()*. This function is called every *loop()* cycle to invert the last LED status, according to the program state (programming, standby, stepper running, etc.)

The Rotary Encoder

To control the rotary encoder, I have used the *ClickEncode* library (https://github.com/robogeek78/SparkCore-ClickEncoder). The advantage of this library is the use of the timer interrupt; so the rotation counter is updated independently by the status of the machine, that is changed accordingly by the interrupt callback function. The main *loop()* function checks the state of the encoder at every cycle as shown below.

```
void loop() {
  // Read the encoder value. Maybe -1, 1 or 0
  radioStepper.encValue = encoder->getValue();

  // Check if the rotary postion has changed (exclude the zero status
  if ( (radioStepper.encValue != 0 ) && (encoderCounter == ENCODER_READINGS)) {
    if(radioStepper.isProgrammed == true) {
      // If the tuner is programmed and the user moves the rotary encoder
      // the programmed status is automatically reset
      setProgrammingStatus(false);
    }
    encoderCounter = 0; // Reset che counter readings
    // Check for the direction (clockwise of conterclockwise)
    if (radioStepper.encValue == ROTARY_CW) {
      radioTuner.step(ONE_MOVE_CLOCKWISE);
      // Update the loop counter (only if programming is set)
      updateLoopCount(ONE_MOVE_CLOCKWISE);
```

```cpp
    } // Clockwise rotation
    else {
      radioTuner.step(ONE_MOVE_COUNTERCLOCKWISE);
      // Update the loop counter (only if programming is set)
      updateLoopCount(ONE_MOVE_COUNTERCLOCKWISE);
      } // Counterclockwise rotation
  } // Rotary encoder has been moved twice
  else {
    if(radioStepper.encValue != 0){
      encoderCounter++;
    }
  } // First encoder reading


  // Check for the rotary encoder button press. The 0 value shown on power-on can't be
selected
  ClickEncoder::Button encButton = encoder->getButton();
  if(encButton == ClickEncoder::Clicked) {
  #ifdef DEBUG
      Serial << "Encoder button clicked" << endl;
  #endif
    if(radioStepper.isSelected == false){
      radioStepper.isSelected = true;
      setProgrammingStatus(false);
      // LED fixed on
      digitalWrite(PROG_LED, HIGH);
#ifdef DEBUG
      Serial << "isSelected true" << endl;
#endif
    } // Button pressed for the first time: start programming the range
    else {
  #ifdef DEBUG
      Serial << "Set prog status true" << endl;
  #endif
      setProgrammingStatus(true);
    } // Programming ended, start looping
  } // Encoder button clicked


  // Check for looping
  if(radioStepper.isLooping == true) {
    radioStepper.tunerPosition += (STEPPER_INCREMENT * radioStepper.loopDirection);
```

```
    // Check if the direction should be inverted
    if( (radioStepper.tunerPosition == 0) || (radioStepper.tunerPosition ==
radioStepper.loopSteps) ) {
        radioStepper.loopDirection *= -1; // Invert the loop direction
    }
    radioTuner.step(STEPPER_INCREMENT * radioStepper.loopDirection);
  }


  // Non-blocking LED blinking, if needed
  blinkLEDOnce();
}
```

There are three status events modified by the rotary encoder: the encoder button pressed, the rotation of the encoder while programming a motion range of the tuner, and the rotation of the encoder when the tuner is programmed.

The Run/Standby Pushbutton

Also, this component acts independently modifying the status of the running program: if the stepper is programmed and the tuner is moving the motor is stopped, and the LED blinks slower; when it is pressed again, the motor restart the rotation sequence.

If the pushbutton is pressed when the stepper motor is not programmed, it does not affect.

The Run/Standby pushbutton is connected the Arduino Nano pin 2 corresponding to the hardware interrupt IRQ_0.

When an interrupt occurs on this pin the callback function *irqLoopButton()* is called automatically regardless of the main loop() execution status.

```
/**
 * IRQ Vector callback for Nano IRQ 0 (the loop control button pin)
 */
void irqLoopButton() {
  if(radioStepper.isProgrammed == true) {
    detachInterrupt(digitalPinToInterrupt(LOOPER_BUTTON));
    // If the tuner is programmed, change the status of the loop flag
    if(radioStepper.isLooping == true) {
      radioStepper.isLooping = false;
```

```
        radioStepper.blinkLEDFrequency = LED_IDLE;
#ifdef DEBUG
        Serial << "LED idle" << endl;
#endif
    } else {
        radioStepper.isLooping = true;
        radioStepper.blinkLEDFrequency = LED_FREQ;
#ifdef DEBUG
        Serial << "LED frequency" << endl;
#endif
    }
  attachInterrupt(digitalPinToInterrupt(LOOPER_BUTTON), irqLoopButton, LOW);
  delay(10);
  radioStepper.millisCounter = millis();
  }
}
```

## CHAPTER 6

The Pi Synth

6.1 Introduction

This project has been introduced in the third Project14 workshop "Vintage Upcycling" by https://www.element14.com/community/events/5617/l/vintage-upcycling-with-raspberry-pi-and-arduino-part-3-1950s-pi-synth?sr=search&searchId=fdd1254e-c5db-4e0a-b77d-d3ed5f3fda22&searchIndex=4

Repository link: https://github.com/alicemirror/RadioMagic

Now that we upcycled a transistor radio to produce sounds; we should sample them and convert to a (sort of) musical instrument.

The Pi Synth project can be called a half-synth. Using a Raspberry Pi I set up as a music machine for sound sampling and MIDI playing, through a virtual interface or a MIDI keyboard connected to the Raspberry Pi. Or both of them.

The application has been developed with Python 3. Also, some hardware improvement has been added to the Pi for better performances and audio sampling.

Good quality sound is better sampled in wav format regardless that this needs more available space. If stressing too much the microSD card reading and writing data, as well as streaming audio, you can damage it and shorten its life. I added a 128 Gb SSD connected to one of the four USB ports of the Raspberry Pi through a SATA-II to USB adapter. The application and the audio files are stored to this external disk leaving only the operating system running on the microSD card.

A panoramic view of the setup of the Pi Synth (on the right side) connected to the Radio Magic.

A further improvement for storage optimisation can be applied moving the Raspbian Linux file system to the SSD disk using microSD only at boot time.

For this version of the project, instead, I have not applied this upgrade. I need to be able to make a copy of the microSD card when the operating system is fully configured.

6.2 Raspberry Pi Audio Sampling and Midi

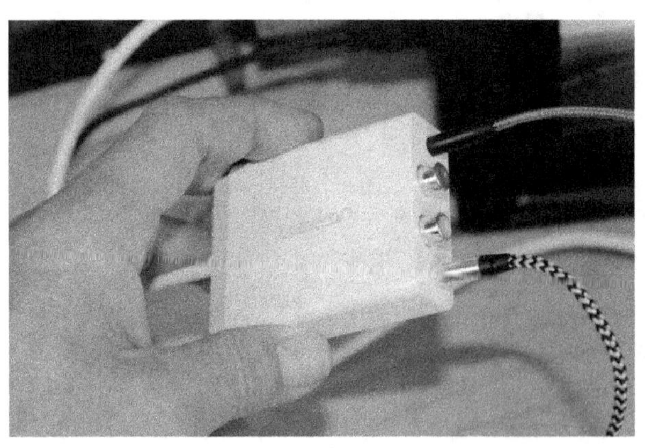

The Ugreen USB audio card used by the Pi Synth.

I could put the hands and experimenting all the Raspberry Pi models, from the first prototype up to the most recent Raspberry Pi 4B model.

The USB Audio Card

While the audio output quality has progressively increased with the evolution of the Raspberry, unfortunately, none of the models included an ADC (Analog to Digital Converter) onboard.

During past years several companies launched on the market audio cards promising high-quality audio sampling. I tested some of these boards, and worked fine; unfortunately, to use these audio devices, it is necessary to install a custom version of the Raspbian Linux

.

The Raspberry Pi audio cards always required dedicated drivers and a modified Linux kernel.

These cards were working only with a certain kernel revision making impossible to upgrade the operating system if card producers was not releasing their custom version of the Linux distribution.

This is the main reason I adopted a different solution.

Excluding very cheap low-quality audio cards, I opted for a good quality USB UGreen card (https://www.ugreen.com/products/usb-audio-adapter-with-3-5mm-2rca). This small device provides monophonic input for sampling, as well as a stereo output, through a couple of 3,5 mm jack plugs. Besides, there are two quality RCA output connectors for external audio (e.g. an amplifier or a mixer).

The installation on the Raspberry Pi is easy; you only need to plug the audio card into one of the Raspberry Pi USB ports and boot the computer. From the audio setting on the Raspberry Pi desktop, the USB audio card appears on the list. The peripheral can play audio as well as recording from an input source using the ALSA drivers.

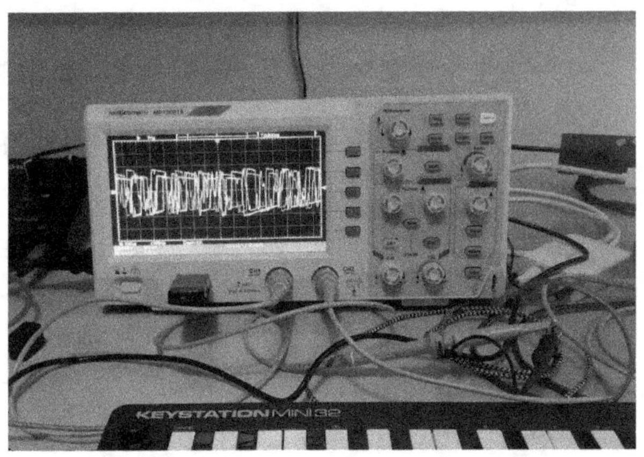

Testing the sampling quality of the audio card with the oscilloscope.

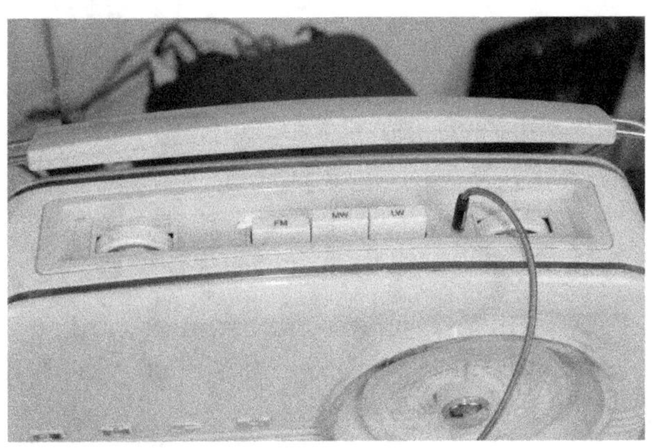

The Radio Magic audio out connected to the Pi Synth for sound sampling.

To test the sampling quality, I connected the input to a frequency generator to generate square and sine waves at different frequencies in the audible range (20-20.000 Hz). Sampling the audio output signal with an oscilloscope from the audio output I verified the stream was identical.

I also repeated the same test with a recorded sound: the differences between the original waves and the recorded file streamed with VLC (Video Lan Converter) were meaningless. The VLC application is included in the standard Raspbian Linux desktop distribution.

Connecting a MDI Keyboard

Though it is not complex to add a standard MIDI port to the Raspberry Pi, I decided to use another USB port as I already own this kind of MIDI keyboard. After connecting the MIDI instrument to one of the Raspberry Pi USB ports, with the terminal command

```
pi@RadioMagic:~ $ cat /proc/asound/cards
```

we get the list of the sound devices connected to the system; in my case, the external peripherals I connected to the Raspberry Pi return the following list:

```
0 [ALSA           ]: bcm2835_alsa - bcm2835 ALSA
                     bcm2835 ALSA
1 [K32            ]: USB-Audio - Keystation Mini 32
                     Keystation Mini 32 Keystation Mini 32 at
usb-3f980000.usb-1.5, full speed
2 [Device         ]: USB-Audio - USB Advanced Audio Device
                     C-Media Electronics Inc. USB Advanced Audio Device
at usb-3f980000.usb-1.3, full speed
```

As listed above the sound card is identified as device 2 while the MIDI keyboard *Keystation Mini 32* is the device 1. Remember this information that will be used to configure the synthesiser.

6.3 Pi Sinth Architecture for First Tests

Before starting to write the program, we should figure out the Pi Synth architecture and design a user interface fast easy to use.

To make some sampling test and become familiar with the newly installed hardware, I installed the Open Source audio editing software Audacity (https://www.audacityteam.org/). It is a very efficient application running fast on the Raspberry Pi, perfect to verifying the features we need in the application.

Audacity is well documented and maintained, an efficient program with the essential features easy to learn.

With Audacity, I tested the Radio Magic connected to the sound card to sample sound sequences.

After saving some audio samples from the Radio Magic, I moved the wav files to play as MIDI notes with the SamplerBox (https://github.com/josephernest/SamplerBox) program.

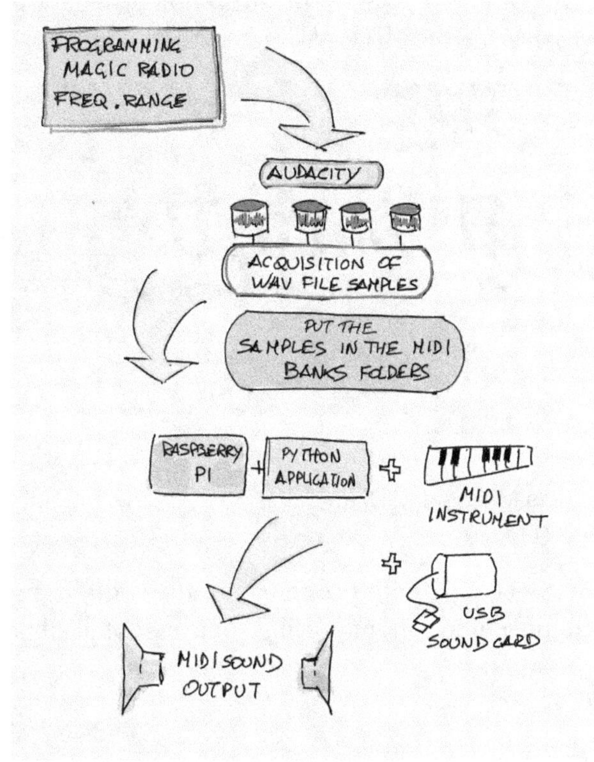

The functional scheme of the test environment.

SamplerBox – actually it is a MIDI player – is an Open Source project developed by the GitHub user josephernest that inspired me to build some parts of the Pi Synth.

The Audio Engine

I found Sampler Box searching on the Internet if someone had already done something similar to what I was thinking to make and, to be honest, I was attracted by the name of the project.

Reading the project details, I saw that had nothing to do with sound sampling but was just a midi player, according to the notes on the GitHub repository and the SamplerBox site (https://www.samplerbox.org/home). There was, instead, a valuable part of the project I used to manage the MIDI playing: the audio engine.

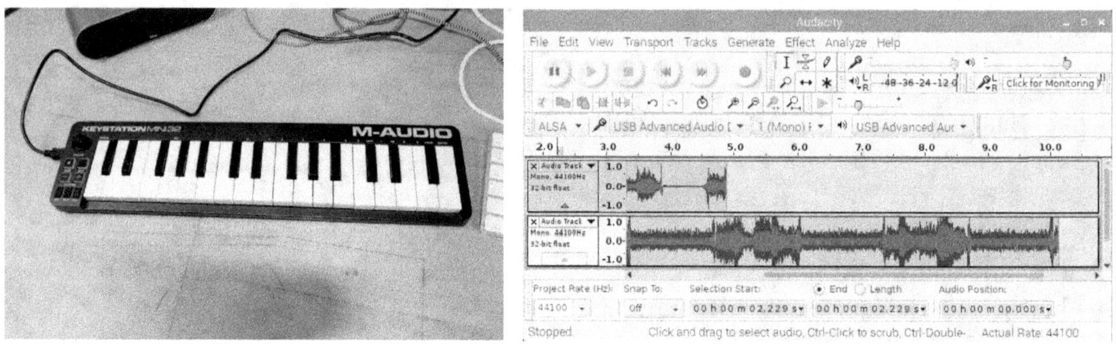

The M-Audio MIDI keyboard used in this project (left) and an example of Audacity audio samples (right).

The Pi Synth program has a very different behaviour, but I have reused the Samples Box audio engine after applying some essential adaptions.

```
##   SamplerBox
#
#  Original audio engine developed by
#  Joseph Ernest (twitter: @JosephErnest, mail: contact@samplerbox.org)
#  license CC3.0 SA
#  (http://creativecommons.org/licenses/by-sa/3.0/)
#
#  samplerbox_audio.pyx: Audio engine for Cython
#
#  Revision: Enrico Miglino <balearicdynamics@gmail.com>
#  Adapted to compile for the Python3 environment
#  Date: September 2020
#  IMPORTANT: Read the setup.py comments on how to setup and compile Cython on Python 3
#
# DO NOT DELETE THE LINE COMMENT BELOW! IT IS A CYTON COMPILER STATEMENT
# cython: language_level=3
```

```python
import cython
import numpy
cimport numpy


def mixaudiobuffers(list playingsounds, list rmlist, int frame_count, numpy.ndarray
FADEOUT, int FADEOUTLENGTH, numpy.ndarray SPEED):
    cdef int i, ii, k, l, N, length, looppos, fadeoutpos
    cdef float speed, newsz, pos, j
    cdef numpy.ndarray b = numpy.zeros(2 * frame_count, numpy.float32)      # output
buffer
    cdef float* bb = <float *> (b.data)                                    # and its
pointer
    cdef numpy.ndarray z
    cdef short* zz
    cdef float* fadeout = <float *> (FADEOUT.data)


    for snd in playingsounds:
        pos = snd.pos
        fadeoutpos = snd.fadeoutpos
        looppos = snd.sound.loop
        length = snd.sound.nframes
        speed = SPEED[snd.note - snd.sound.midinote]
        newsz = frame_count * speed
        z = snd.sound.data
        zz = <short *> (z.data)

        N = frame_count

        if ( (pos + frame_count * speed > length - 4) and (looppos == -1) ):
            rmlist.append(snd)
            N = <int> ((length - 4 - pos) / speed)

        if (snd.isfadeout):
            if (fadeoutpos > FADEOUTLENGTH):
                rmlist.append(snd)
            ii = 0
            for i in range(N):
                j = pos + ii * speed
                ii += 1
                k = <int> j
```

```
            if (k > length - 2):
                pos = looppos + 1
                snd.pos = pos
                ii = 0
                j = pos + ii * speed
                k = <int> j
            bb[2 * i] += (zz[2 * k] + (j - k) * (zz[2 * k + 2] - zz[2 * k])) *
fadeout[fadeoutpos + i]                     # linear interpolation
            bb[2 * i + 1] += (zz[2 * k + 1] + (j - k) * (zz[2 * k + 3] - zz[2 * k +
1])) * fadeout[fadeoutpos + i]
        snd.fadeoutpos += i


    else:
        ii = 0
        for i in range(N):
            j = pos + ii * speed
            ii += 1
            k = <int> j
            if (k > length - 2):
                pos = looppos + 1
                snd.pos = pos
                ii = 0
                j = pos + ii * speed
                k = <int> j
            bb[2 * i] += zz[2 * k] + (j - k) * (zz[2 * k + 2] - zz[2 * k])
# linear interpolation
            bb[2 * i + 1] += zz[2 * k + 1] + (j - k) * (zz[2 * k + 3] - zz[2 * k + 1])

        snd.pos += ii * speed


    return b


def binary24_to_int16(char *data, int length):
    cdef int i
    res = numpy.zeros(length, numpy.int16)
    b = <char *>((<numpy.ndarray>res).data)
    for i in range(length):
        b[2*i] = data[3*i+1]
        b[2*i+1] = data[3*i+2]
    return res
```

As shown in the above code, the audio engine is written in Python (the original version was Python 2.,7 that I ported to Python 3). The few functions defined in this script should be highly performant and reactive, so the Python source has been cythonized.

Instead of the ".py" file extension, this source file has been assigned the ".pyx" extension.

What is Cython

Cython (*https://cython.org/*) is a tool to optimise the Python code, including the external libraries and generating a C source further compiled as a static object. During this optimisation process, Cython includes the wrapper to be able to include the compiled – faster and faster – C component in the Python scripts as well as including a Python class or library.

To install the tool on the Raspberry Pi it is sufficient to launch the command

```
$>pip3 install Cython
```

After the installation of Cython, the source can be Cythonized. Below some useful notes on compiling Python3 sources on the Raspbian Linux Buster distribution. Resuming, below the compile notes included in the setup.py program to compile the audio engine (available on the project GitHub repository)

```
1. Install Cython with

        $>pip3 install cython

2. Check that the installed version if 2.29 or higher, with the command
$>cython -V

        If Cython was already installed with a previous version, upgrade
Cython for Python 3

        to the last available version in the repository with the command

        $>pip3 install --upgrade cython

        Check the version again.

3. Add the comment

        #cython: language_level=3

special setting in the comments on top of the pyx source

This set the language level of the compiler globally for all the
sources
```

If you are compiling multiple sources, and only some of these are Python 3, instead,

you should use the settings for language level only for those sources.

For more details read the Cyton documentations:

https://cython.readthedocs.io/en/latest/src/userguide/
migrating_to_cy30.html?highlight=python%203

4. If you need to import the C libraries of numpy there is a workaound that should

be applied to make the compilation working in the SPECIFIC CASE OF RASPBERRY PI if during the compilation

you get an error like

libf77blas.so.3: cannot open shared object file: No such file or directory

at the end of a series of compilation errors that involves numpy.

As described in the Numpy troubleshooting documentation

https://numpy.org/devdocs/user/troubleshooting-importerror.html

this is due to a missing library that should be installed from the Raspbian repositories with the command

$>sudo apt-get install libatlas-base-dev

This issue should be avoided also installing numpy with the Raspbian if the version if recent. Try before

with Buster distro or next ones, with the command

$>pip3 uninstall numpy

$>sudo apt install python3-numpy

6.4 The User Interface

The user interface should follow some guidelines:

- Use only touch buttons, no mouse or settings are needed
- Adopt a simple colour coding
- Match the MIDI logic (notes, octaves, sound banks)
- Should be highly responsive
- Should be parametric
- Can be represented on the 7" Raspberry Pi touch screen

This list of requirements has conditioned both the design itself and the graphical tool I have used to achieve the goal.

The button grid represents from left to right, a full twelve notes octave, from C to B. From top to bottom every row is of the eight octaves covering the full extension of the MIDI. The remaining rightmost four columns are reserved to the synth commands.

There is still an improvement I planned to do in the future: adding a row header with the note names and a left column with the octaves numbers.

Coding the User Interface

To make the user interface as described above, I used TkInter (https://wiki.python.org/moin/TkInter). It is the Python standard GUI package based on TCL/Tk (http://www.tcl.tk/) language. Developed in TCL Tk makes it possible to design interfaces on any kind of platform.

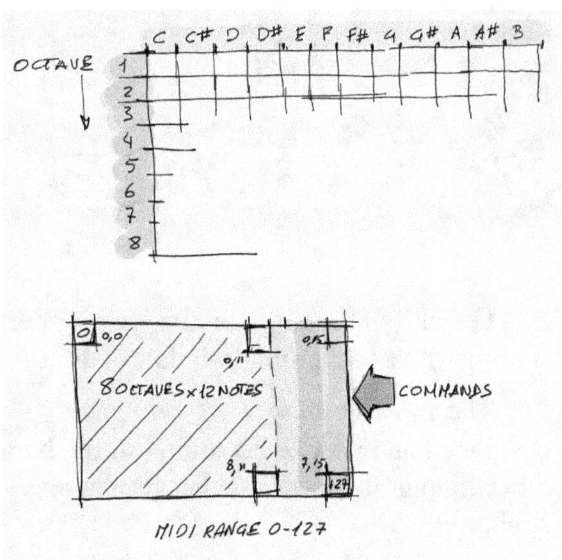

The user interface buttons grid and the reference to the MIDI 128 possible values.

Tk is a graphical user interface toolkit that takes developing desktop applications to a higher level than conventional approaches. Tk is the standard GUI not only for Tcl, but for many other dynamic languages, and can produce rich, native applications that run unchanged across Windows, Mac OS X, Linux and more.

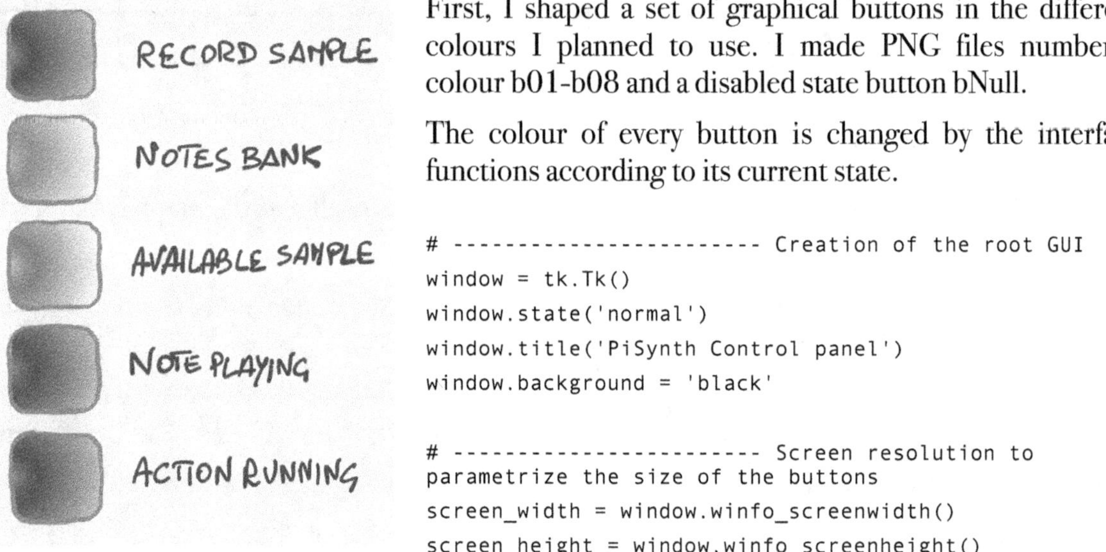

First, I shaped a set of graphical buttons in the different colours I planned to use. I made PNG files numbered colour b01-b08 and a disabled state button bNull.

The colour of every button is changed by the interface functions according to its current state.

```
# ----------------------- Creation of the root GUI
window = tk.Tk()
window.state('normal')
window.title('PiSynth Control panel')
window.background = 'black'


# ----------------------- Screen resolution to
parametrize the size of the buttons
screen_width = window.winfo_screenwidth()
screen_height = window.winfo_screenheight()
```

On start of the program the GUI is created defining an instance of the Tk Python library starting with a background window of the same size of the screen.

The *function load_GUI_parameters()* create the interface components parametrically positioned and resided according to the buttons size and the screen dimensions. A series of other graphical functions change che state of the buttons depending on the state of the application.

```
def load_GUI_parameters():
    '''

    Load the GUI parameters from the gui.json file and create the
    buttons image list and the frame to include the buttons
    '''

    # Buttons grid size, rows
```

```
global panel_rows
# Buttons grid size, columns
global panel_cols
# Number of images (shaded colors) a button can have
global max_button_images
# The max number of function groups (associated to the same number of
# button colors)
global max_button_functions
# The size of the square buttons
global button_size
# Full path of the samples (bank folders)
global samples_path
# Full path of the GUI images
global images_path
# Image files extension (jpeg or png)
global image_extension
# Buttons images list
# Every button can assume one of the images in the list, according
# to the applicaiton logic
# The button images are named accordingly, in the format b<nn>.png
global b_images
# button image without associated functio
global image_off_button
# The frame that includes all the buttons.
# The parameters for the border and pads will center the button grid
# on the screen. Keep them fixed! Should be recalculated if the
# button size or number of buttons change.
global frame_container
# Frame container border
global f_border
# Frame container pad x
global f_padx
# Frame container pad y
global f_pady
# Ma value for pholyphony output
# This can be set higher, but 80 is a safe value
global max_polyphony
# The ID of the audio output device. In the case of the internal output it is
# 0 or 1 depending on the setting of analog output or HDMI output. The USB
```

```python
# sound board has typically the id 2
global audio_device_id
# List with the names of the notes to load the samples
# Every sample file name is the same of the note that should
# associated in the selected bank. The missing notes are
# calculated expanding and compressing the sample frequencies
global note_names
# Midi device name as it appears in the list of recognized
# midi devices connected to the USB
global midi_device
# Recording sample rate (44 or 48 KHz
global sampling_rate
# Recording chunk size in bytes (will work fine with 4096)
global recording_chunk_size
# Recording channels. Currently only the mono recording is
# supported by the audio card (1 channel)
global input_channels
# The current status of the system
global synth_Status
# The sample record duration (seconds)
# The value should be included between 1 sec and 9 sec max.
global sample_lenght
# The fade out duration base for the notes. This value is
# used to calculate the fadeout of every note
global FADEOUTLENGTH
# Note fadeout
global FADEOUT
# Playing speed (stretch factore)
global SPEED


# Loads the parameters main dictionary
with open("gui.json") as file:
    dictionary = json.load(file)


# Interface settings
image_extension = dictionary['imageType']
images_path = dictionary['images']
max_button_images = int(dictionary['buttonImages'])
max_button_functions = max_button_images
```

```python
samples_path = dictionary['samples']
panel_rows = int(dictionary['rows'])
panel_cols = int(dictionary['columns'])
button_size = dictionary['buttonsize']
f_border = int(dictionary['frame_border'])
f_padx = int(dictionary['frame_padX'])
f_pady = int(dictionary['frame_padY'])

# Playing control parameters
max_polyphony = int(dictionary['maxPolyphony'])
audio_device_id = int(dictionary['audioDevice'])
midi_device = dictionary['midiDevice']
note_names = dictionary['note_names']

# Recording settings
sampling_rate = int(dictionary['recordSampleRate'])
recording_chunk_size = int(dictionary['recordChunkSize'])
input_channels = int(dictionary['recordChannels'])
sample_lenght = int(dictionary['recordDuration'])

# Check to the sample lenght limits
if(sample_lenght < 1):
    sample_lenght = 1
elif(sample_lenght > 9):
    sample_lenght = 9

# Initial status when starting
synth_Status = PiSynthStatus.STANDBY

# Read the global fadeout duration and calculate
# the notes fadeout
FADEOUTLENGTH = int(dictionary['fadeoutLength'])
FADEOUT = Utilities.calcFade1(FADEOUTLENGTH)
FADEOUT = Utilities.calcFade2(FADEOUT)
FADEOUT = Utilities.calcFade3(FADEOUT, FADEOUTLENGTH)

SPEED = Utilities.calcStretchFactor()

# The frame that includes all the buttons.
```

```python
    # The parameters for the border and pads will center the button grid
    # on the screen. Keep them fixed! Should be recalculated if the
    # button size or number of buttons change.
    frame_container = create_frame_container()

    # Pack the frame container ready to include the buttons grid
    frame_container.pack(
        side=tk.TOP,
        fill=tk.BOTH
    )


    # Prepares the images for the graphic interface
    image_off_button = resize_image_button(images_path + dictionary['offButtonImage'] +
image_extension)
    b_images = list(resize_image_button((images_path + "b%02d" + image_extension) % (i +
1))
                    for i in range(max_button_images))
```

The number of buttons, rows, columns, and the other parameters of the interface are defined in the file *gui.json* together with the other parameters of the application.

6.5 Sampling and Playing

Completing the user interface has been one of the difficult parts of Pi Synth. After the buttons grid worked as expected, I connected the GUI to the features of the program.

The MIDI Keyboard

The MIDI keyboard events are intercepted by the program through the MidiCallback() function shown below.

When a MIDI event occurs this function extract the MIDI components of the message and executes the corresponding sound of the selected octave.

When a note button press is detected, it is interpreted in the same way like on the MIDI keyboard. Working through interrupts multiple MIDI messages are accepted at the same time, also mixing MIDI keyboard and interface buttons.

The Sound Samples

It is possible to record multiple sound samples associated with the notes of the desired octave. This is the case, for example, when acquiring different radio sequences to be played associated with a series of keys (notes).

However, this process is not indispensable to generate the sounds of a full octave. If a single sample is acquired to be associated with the first note of an octave the remaining 11 notes are automatically generated stretching the wav file accordingly.

The samples are organised in banks. Every bank should be a folder following a simple naming convention: b0 for bank number 1 up to b7 for bank number 8. The banks' folders contain the sample wav files where the file name corresponds to the note and octave the sample is associated. For example, the 'C' note of bank number 3 is a file named C3.wav.

If a note sample already exists when a new sample is saved, the previous file is overwritten. It is also possible to configure some playing characteristics for every bank editing the content of one of the eight bank configuration json files. Also, the json files follow the same naming convention of the bank folders: from bank0.json for the bank number1 up to bank7.json for bank number 8. Below an example of a bank configuration file.

```
{
    "volume" : 1.0,
    "transpose" : 0,
    "velocity" : 64
}
```

The Application Configuration File

The *gui.json* file defines all the parameters of the Pi Synth. The samples folder path makes it easy to move the sound samples to different locations without changing the program. The two parameters midiDevice and audioDevice are used to open the external sound card and the midi device connected to the Raspberry Pi.

The list note_names is used for the MIDI message decoding, as well as creating the right wav file name when sampling.

The recordSampleRate defines the quality of the audio sampling; this value should be set according to the characteristics of the audio card and should match the hardware configuration.

The recordDuration parameter defines the number of seconds to acquire the samples always the same for all the banks. Take care to limit this value to 10 seconds max, to avoid memory errors.

```
{
  "samples": "/media/pi/EXTERNAL/controlpanel/Samples/",
  "images": "/media/pi/EXTERNAL/controlpanel/images/",
  "rows" : 8,
  "columns" : 16,
  "buttonImages" : 8,
  "buttonsize" : 44,
  "frame_padX" : 0,
  "frame_padY" : 0,
  "frame_border" : 0,
  "offButtonImage" : "bNull",
  "imageType" : ".png",
  "audioDevice" : 2,
  "midiDevice" : "Keystation Mini 32 20:0",
  "maxPolyphony" : 80,
  "note_names" : [  "c", "c#", "d", "d#", "e", "f", "f#", "g", "g#", "a", "a#", "b" ],
  "recordSampleRate" : 44100,
  "recordChunkSize" : 4096,
  "recordChannels" : 1,
  "recordDuration" : 5,
  "fadeoutLength" : 30000
}
```

Recording a Sample

The sample recording procedure can be executed at any moment for any note of the current bank. It is sufficient:

- The light blue button in the rightmost column shows the currently selected bank. Press the left side blue button that changes to red.

- Press the desired note (column) in the selected octave (row) to start sampling.

- When the sample ends the red button is back to blue.

As the recording ends, the note is immediately available for playing; the previously recorded note, if any, is overwritten by the new sample. If the sample has been recorded in a free position (grey button) the colour changes to yellow.

## CHAPTER 7

The Vintage Synth

7.1 The Reason Why

This is an unpublished project, presented for the first time on this book.

Repository link: https://github.com/alicemirror/RadioMagic

The idea of making a Vintage synthesiser was born while upcycling the Radio Magic and the Pi Synth. Instead of upcycling a vintage device with modern electronics, the Vintage Synth tries to approach the analogue synth technology using vintage components by adding some improvements using modern technologies and microcontrollers.

This project smoothly integrates the Radio Magic – a sampling device – with the Pi Synth, a Linux machine to make music.

The sounds generated by the Vintage Synth is purely analogue: the core is an astable oscillator interfering with another oscillator set in PWM mode. This simple module, based on a couple of NE555 and some discrete components are replicated three times so that the oscillators can be set to resonate together in several ways.

The sound of the three synth modules is mixed to a single output signal. The mixing module also accepts a fourth input coming from the Radio Magic.

This is the last project of the book that reverts the roles: instead of upcycling an old electronics, it is an old electronic technology made in the actual days.

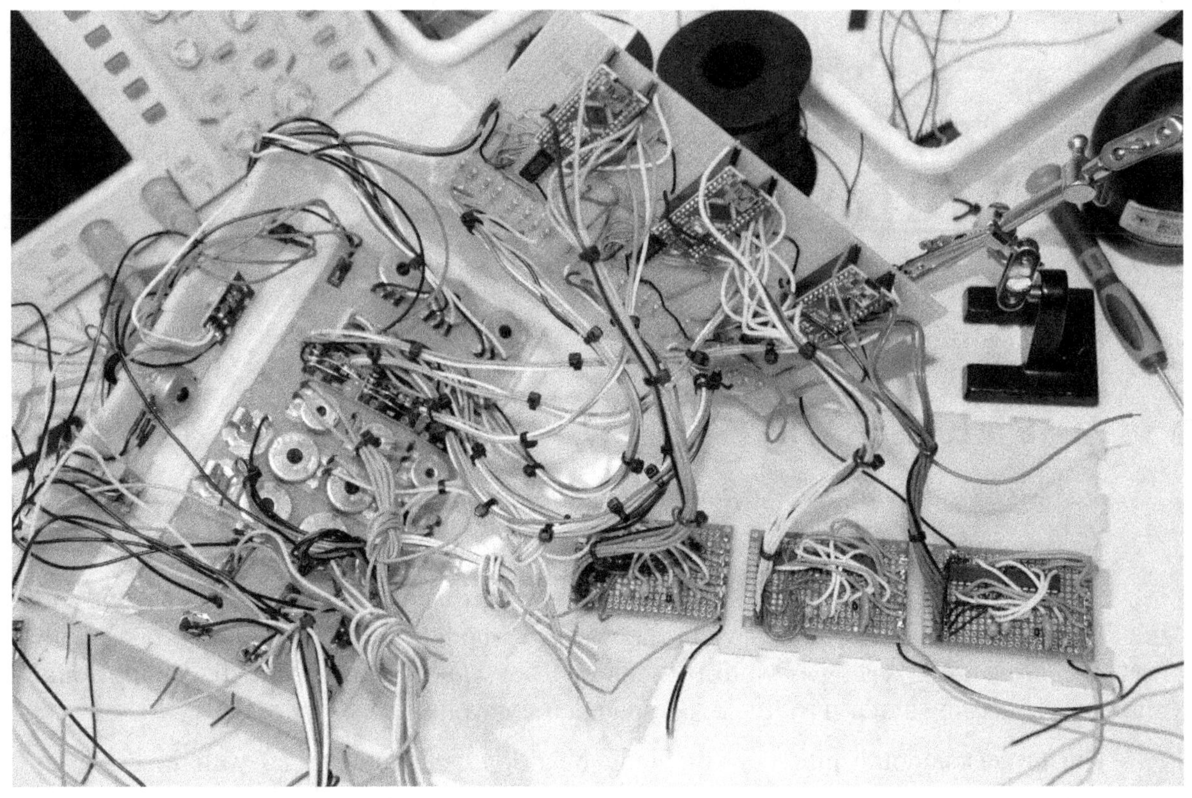

The first Vintage Synth prototype.

Indeed, I have not yet found a case for the build as I am searching for a nice Vintage object that can be modified to host the Vintage Synth boards.A Modular System

For this project, I started working around the circuit of the two oscillators, then I thought about how it was possible to improve the first circuit in some way. Creating multiple units of the same set has been the next step.

7.2 The Synth Module

As I always do, the first step has been breadboarding the two oscillators circuit to verify that it was possible to produce good sounds.

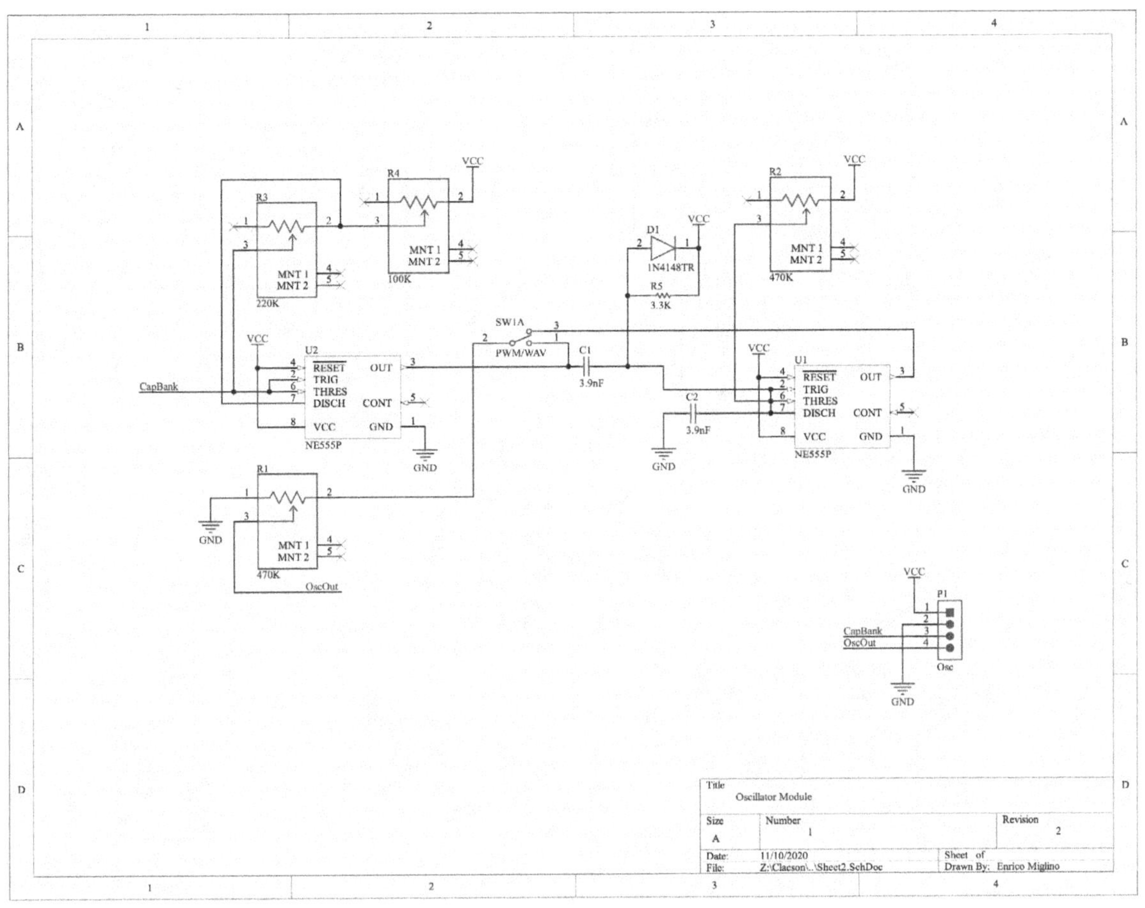

The schematics of the oscillator module created with Altium Designer.

According to the schematics above the NE555 U2 generates a waveform altered by the two potentiometers R3 and R4.

The NE555 U1 instead generates a PWM pulse (Pulse With Modulation) that change the square waveform generated by U2, while through the switch SW1A it is possible to enable or disable this feature.

The frequency range generated by the circuit of U2 is defined by the value of the capacitor connected to the CapBank input.

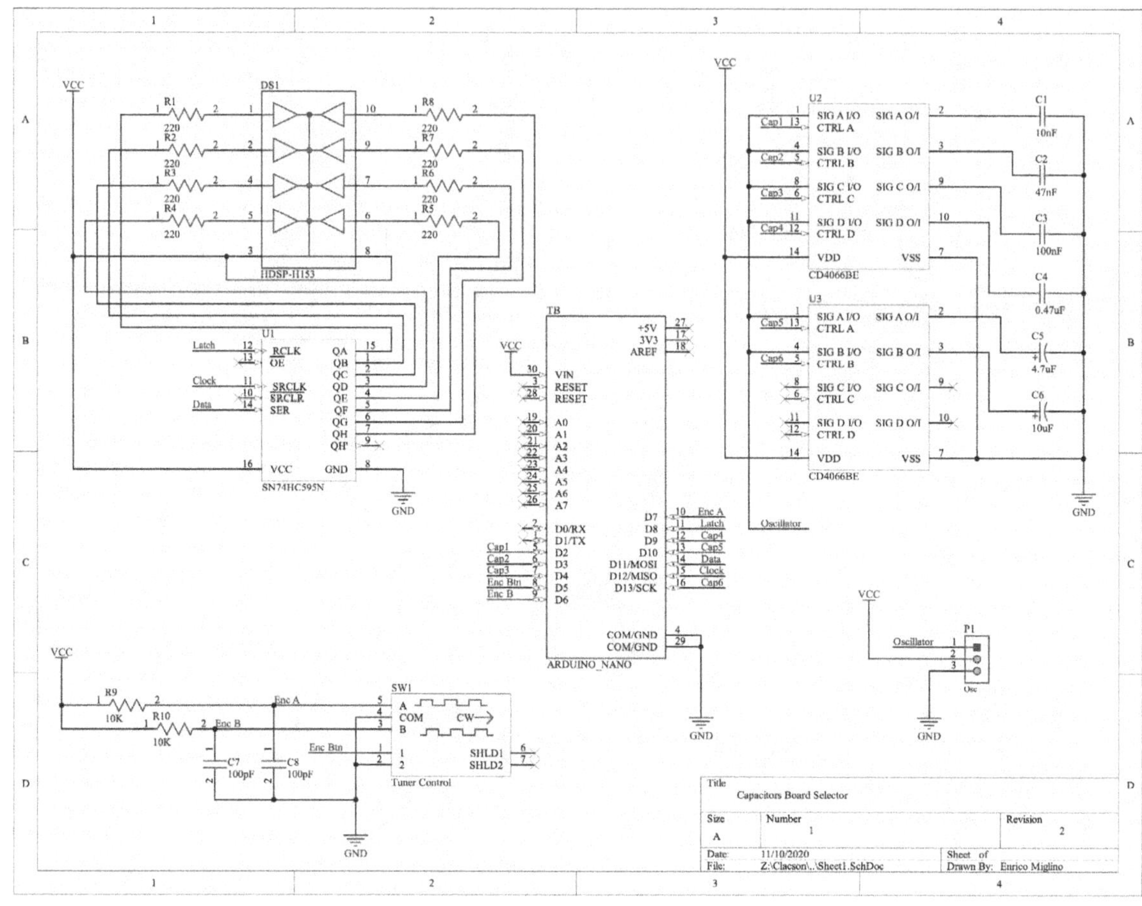

The schematic of the capacitors bank selector made with Altium Designer.

7.3 The Capacitors Bank

Changing the value of the capacitor the range of frequency changes as well.

Instead of a fixed capacitor, I designed another module to be able to change the capacitor value from and external control.

To achieve this goal I designed a circuit using an Arduino Nano to select one from a bank of six capacitors with a rotary encoder.

The logic of the circuit is simple: an Arduino Nano controls the selection of the desired capacitor from a series of six according to the number selected with a rotary encoder.

The number is shown on a seven-segments LED, single-digit display.

In practice, things are a bit complex as I wanted to keep the synthesiser fully analogue.

Using two analogue switches 4066BE the resulting effect is like the capacitor is selected with a manual switch.

Due to the limited number of GPIO pins of the Arduino Nano, I had to limit the number of capacitors to six though the two 4066BE can control up to 8 analogue switches. The seven-segments LED digit is controlled through a 74HC595N shift register consuming only three pins of the Arduino Nano GPIO.

The Arduino Nano Sketch

The sketch of the capacitors bank selector module is derived by the Radio Magic software to control the rotary encoder. This part is almost identical but, instead of controlling the stepper motor, the rotary encoder only changes the number shown on the seven-segments LED digit.

```
/**
 * Main loop function
 *
 * @note The rotary counter should be read twice before the number is incremented
 * due to the mechanical characterisics of the device: it is difficult to positio
 * the encoder in the intermediate positionl
 */
int encoderCounter = 0;

void loop() {
  // Read the encoder value. Maybe -1, 1 or 0
  bankCapacitors.encValue = encoder->getValue();

  // Check if the rotary postion has changed (exclude the zero status
  if ( (bankCapacitors.encValue != 0 ) && (encoderCounter == ENCODER_READINGS)) {
    // Disable the bank selection until the user does not press the rotary encoder button
    encoderCounter = 0; // Reset che counter readings
```

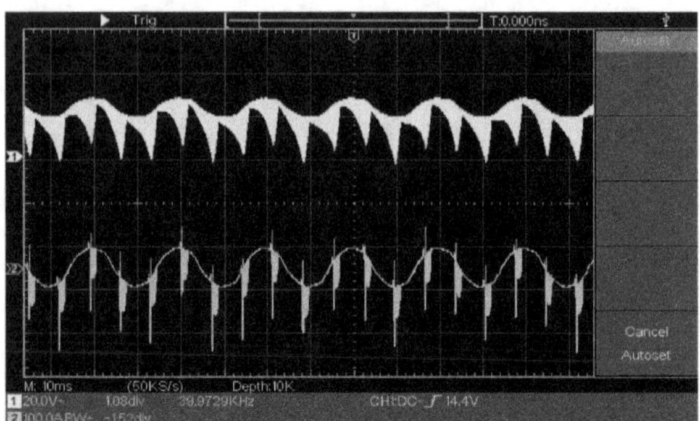

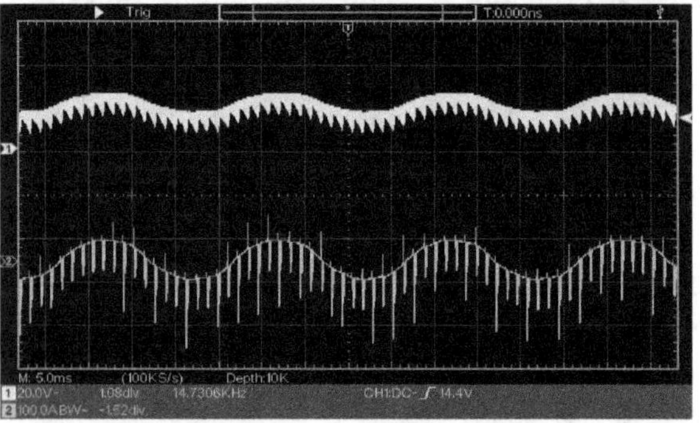

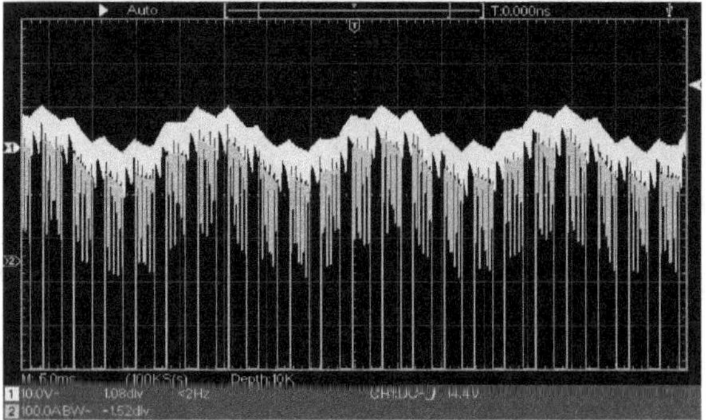

Three examples of the waveform generated by the synth oscillators: the yellow track is generated by the astable oscillator while the blue track is generated by the second one configured in PWM mode.

```
} // First encoder reading
```

```
    bankCapacitors.isSelected = false;
    // Disable all the capacitors until a new one is not selected
    disableAllCaps();
    // Check for the direction (clockwise of conterclockwise)
    if (bankCapacitors.encValue == ROTARY_CW) {
      // Clockwise rotation, update the number by 1
      bankCapacitors.currentBank++;
      if(bankCapacitors.currentBank > NUM_CAPACITORS) {
        bankCapacitors.currentBank = 1;
      }
      #ifdef DEBUG
      Serial << "Clockwise rotation " << bankCapacitors.currentBank << endl;
      #endif
    } // Clockwise rotation
    else {
      bankCapacitors.currentBank--;
      if(bankCapacitors.currentBank < 1) {
        bankCapacitors.currentBank = NUM_CAPACITORS;
      }
      #ifdef DEBUG
      Serial << "Counterclockwise rotation " << bankCapacitors.currentBank << endl;
      #endif
    } // Counterclockwise rotation
  update7Seg();
} // Rotary encoder has been moved twice
else {
  if(bankCapacitors.encValue != 0){
    encoderCounter++;
    #ifdef DEBUG
    Serial << "First encoder reading" << endl;
    #endif
  }
```

```
  // Check for the rotary encoder button press. The 0 value shown on power-on can't be
selected
  ClickEncoder::Button encButton = encoder->getButton();
  if( (encButton == ClickEncoder::Clicked) &&
      (bankCapacitors.isSelected == false) &&
      (bankCapacitors.currentBank > 0) ) {
    #ifdef DEBUG
    Serial << "BUTTON PRESSED " << endl;
    #endif
    bankCapacitors.isSelected = true;
    update7Seg();
    enableCap();
  }
}
```

As the user starts rotating the knob of the encoder the currently selected capacitor, if any, is disabled, and the corresponding synth oscillator stops generating the waveform.

When the number corresponds to the desired capacitor value, pressing the knob button of the encoder the corresponding capacitor is connected to the analogue circuit through the 4066 analogue switch.

Rotating the encoder is also a fast method for silencing the corresponding synth module without changing the volume level.

Assembling and programming the capacitor bank selector on the PCB created with Altium Designer.

```
//! Update the 7-segments LED display according to the number index of the array
//! If the bank selected flag is enabled, the dot is shown as well.
void update7Seg() {
  // Update the number on the display
  regOne.pinOff(0xFF);
  // Check for the Dot
  if(bankCapacitors.isSelected == true) {
    regOne.pinOn(0xFF - (segments[bankCapacitors.currentBank] + segments[DOT_7SEG]) );
  } else {
    regOne.pinOn(0xFF - segments[bankCapacitors.currentBank] );
  }
}
```

The function update7Seg() changes the status of the seven segments digit according to the position of the rotary encoder, while the two funcions disableAllCaps() and enableCap() shown below control the status of the capacitors bank.

```
void disableAllCaps() {
  for(int j = 0; j < NUM_CAPACITORS; j++) {
    digitalWrite(capArray[j], LOW);
  }
}

void enableCap() {
  disableAllCaps();
  digitalWrite(capArray[bankCapacitors.currentBank - 1], HIGH);
}
```

The three capacitors bank selector modules and the synth modules while assembling the synth.

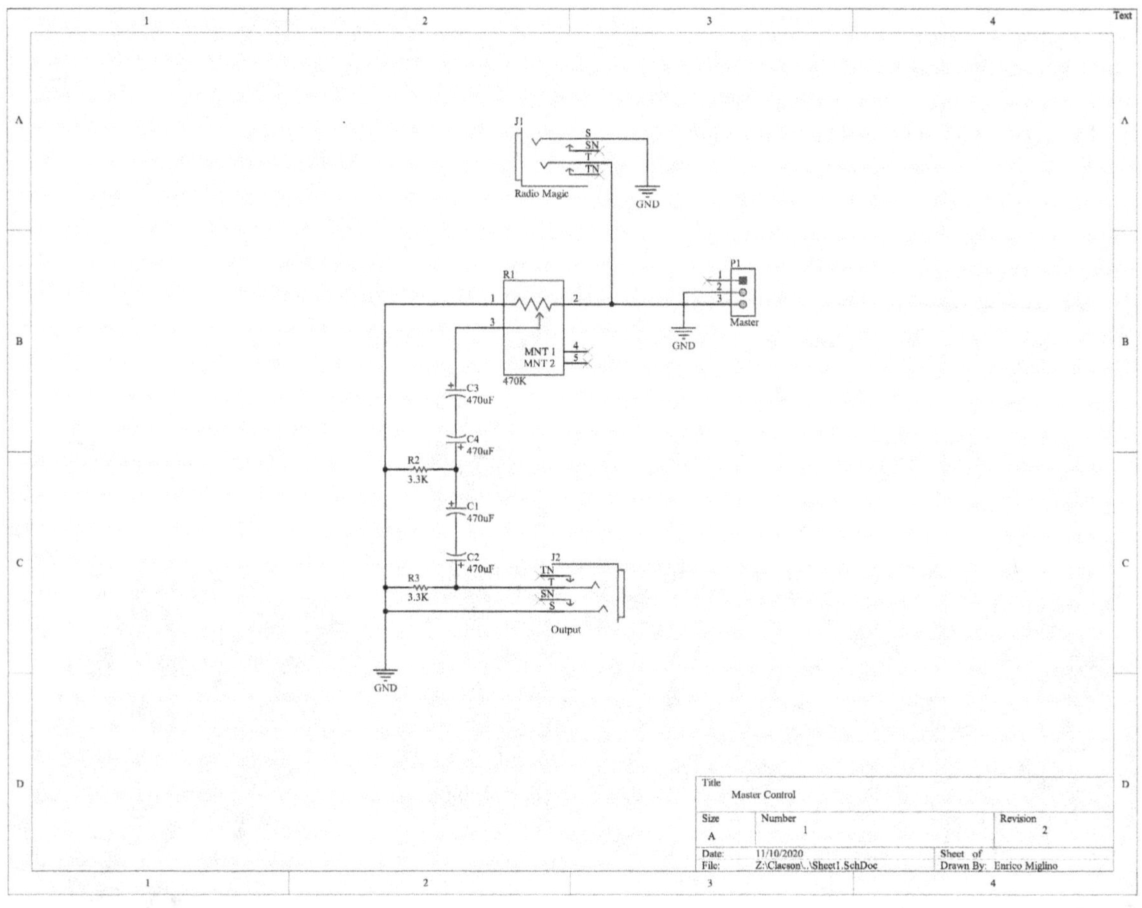

The schematic of the mixer module created with Altium Designer.

7.4 The Other Modules

The third kind of module, also exclusively based on analogue, discrete components is the mixer collecting the output of up to three synth modules (a couple of synth and capacitors bank selector).

This module can accept a fourth external input thought for the Radio Magic sampling device through a 6.5 mm Jack and exposes a monophonic output through a second 6.5 mm

The Vintage Synth modules connected and working. All the PCB and circuits of this project have been created with Altium Designer.

Jack. It also includes a global volume potentiometer.

To work as I expected the Vintage Synth modules should be connected together.

To minimize the wiring and keep the design clean, I also designed a connector module to host the three synth modules, their respective capacitors bank selector and the mixing module.

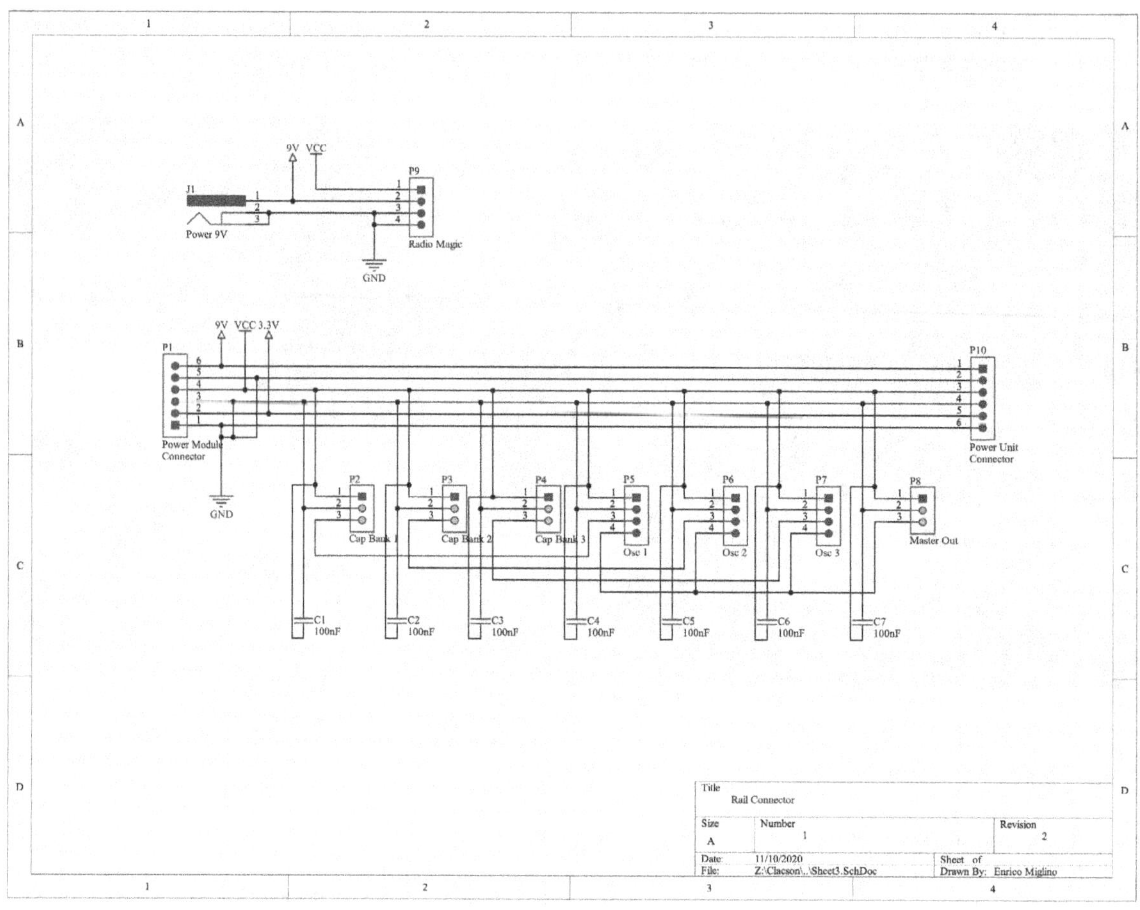

The schematic of the rail connector created with Altium Designer.

Note that the 100nF capacitors between the Vcc and GND remove potential noise in the signals.

There is an extra 9V power line is needed for future usage; the unregulated power line from the power plug to the Radio Magic connector is specific for powering the Radio Magic transistor board replacing the original battery.

With this solution also the Radio Magic board can be included in the same case of the Vintage Synth.

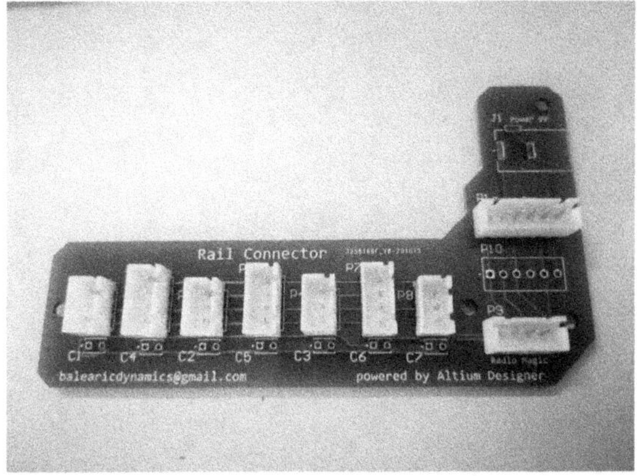

The synth mixer module (left) and the rail connector of theVintage Synth (right).

Finished to write, November 10th, 2020